MAKING
DOLLS' HOUSES
for Children

MAKING
DOLLS' HOUSES
for Children

Vic Campden

LOCHAR PUBLISHING
MOFFAT . SCOTLAND

1991

Published by Lochar Publishing Ltd.
MOFFAT DG10 9ED

British Library Cataloguing in Publication Data

Campden, Vic

Making dolls' houses for children.

1. Dolls' Houses. Making

I. Title

745.5923.

ISBN 0-948403-44-6

Typeset in 12/14pt and 10/12pt Goudy by
Hewer Text Composition Services and printed
in Great Britain by Eagle Colourbooks.

Plans by Vic Campden
Photographs by Zvonko Krachun

*To my grandchildren
Suzie, Steven and Rhiannon*

CONTENTS

Introduction

SECTION 1
Tools and Materials

11

SECTION 2
Construction Details

18

SECTION 3
Toy Making Projects

28

PROJECT 1
Castle 'Flat-Pack'

30

PROJECT 2
'Cottage' Dolls' House

37

PROJECT 3
Garage and Filling Station

46

PROJECT 4
'Woodland Cottage' Dolls' House

57

PROJECT 5
'Gables' Dolls' House

65

PROJECT 6
A Zoo

78

PROJECT 7
'Bay Windows' Dolls' House

88

PROJECT 8
Georgian Dolls' House

102

PROJECT 9
A Farm

116

PROJECT 10
The Corner Shop

127

PROJECT 11
Dolls' House Furniture

139

PROJECT 12
Tudor Dolls' House

151

INTRODUCTION

I t cannot be denied that there are some very good commercially made toys on the market today, but the majority are mass-produced with an extensive use of plastic in their manufacture. Well-made wooden toys, especially dolls' houses, are very expensive, doubtless because of the labour costs involved. It is not difficult to make wooden toys once the fairly simple skills and techniques of using woodworking tools have been mastered, and the satisfaction of completing a well-made toy is a justifiable emotion, especially when it is seen to bring so much pleasure to the child recipient.

The prime purpose of this book is to introduce the beginner to the pleasurable pastime of making wooden toys, but even the more experienced craftsman or woman may gain some snippets of useful information from the tips and hints given and which have been are the result of years of practical experience.

Additionally, the toy-making projects which are included in the book can be useful to the experienced as well as to the beginner. The fact that their construction details have been fully described and dimensioned is not only essential for the beginner but must also be very helpful for the more experienced woodworker. Nothing can be more exasperating than to attempt to work to badly drawn and incorrectly dimensioned details, often given in what otherwise might be excellent publications.

The first two sections of this book are intended to provide helpful information concerning tools and materials, and construction advice. The third section contains a number of toy-making projects and it takes up the larger part of the book, as it should do. After all, the purpose of the book is to enable the reader to make wooden toys and there is no better way of learning the craft than to gain the practical experience of actually making them.

SECTION 1

TOOLS AND MATERIALS

T his section of the book is intended to provide advice on the tools and materials which are needed for the construction of the projects described in Section 3.

It is considered that most people are familiar with the use of the more common woodworking tools such as saws, hammers and screwdrivers. Accordingly, the advice given is confined to those tools which are not so common, especially to the beginner, and which are employed for the cutting, shaping and joining of plywood, this being the prime material used in the making of the toys.

TOOLS

The work bench

For the work required to shape and form plywood a heavy carpenter's bench is not essential. The main requirement is for a worktop to which a cutting table (see later) can be attached.

An adequate and versatile bench is the commercially available 'workmate' which can be folded away when not in use and the top of which can be manipulated to provide a very useful vice or grip for holding work between the edges of its two adjustable bench-top parts.

The working life of this bench can be usefully extended by making a sturdy cover to protect its top when using if for hammering, drilling, or other damaging tasks. A piece of 25 mm (1 in)

thick blockboard or plywood is cut to a size equal to the length of the bench and equal to its width in the closed position *plus* 50 mm (2 in). Fix to the underside of the board a 50 × 25 mm (2 × 1 in) batten of equal length to the board (*Fig. 1*) The board sits securely on the bench with the batten clamped between the two parts of its top.

The fretsaw

This hand-tool is ideal for cutting sheet timber, especially plywood, into any shape required.

It has two limitations. The first is the length of cut which can be made into a piece of wood (work-piece) and which is limited by the saw frame size, i.e. the distance between the saw blade and the back of the frame, usually either 304 mm (12 in) or 406 mm (16 in). For this reason it is recommended that the larger sized

frame be obtained. Longer cuts can be achieved by cutting the maximum length from one direction and completing the cut by approaching it from the opposite direction. In this way a maximum cut of twice the frame size should be possible but in practice a cut somewhat shorter than the possible maximum is the manageable limit. For this reason all the projects described in this book are well within the limitations for cutting with a 406 mm (16 in) frame. The second limitation is the thickness of wood which can be cut with a hand held fretsaw. With care and patience wood of a thickness of 18 mm ($\frac{3}{4}$ in) can be cut but any thickness up to 12 mm ($\frac{1}{2}$ in) should cut without undue difficulty. The important thing is to use a blade of the correct grade. Blades of various grades from 00 (for thin sheet and fine work) up to 11 (for thicker sheet and coarser cuts) are available. Three grades meet most requirements – grade 2 for cutting up to 4 mm ($\frac{1}{8}$ in) thickness,

grade 4 for thicknesses over 4 mm ($\frac{1}{8}$ in) up to 6 mm ($\frac{1}{4}$ in), and grade 6 for thicknesses over 6 mm ($\frac{1}{4}$ in) up to 18 mm ($\frac{3}{4}$ in).

The technique of using a fretsaw is to hold the saw with its blade in a vertical position and to use steady strokes without applying undue pressure of the blade against the work-piece. The cutting stroke is the downward stroke and for this reason the blade must be inserted with its teeth facing forwards and downwards.

The saw should be held in a constant directional position and the work-piece should be rotated when a change of cutting direction is required, rather than to alter the direction in which the saw is facing. When negotiating the cut of an angled corner, keep the saw blade moving (up and down) at the point of the corner whilst rotating the work-piece into a position for the next line of cut.

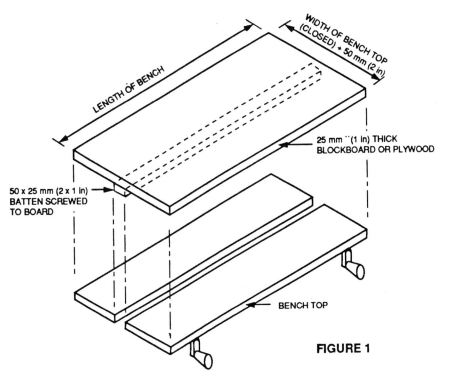

25 mm ``(1 in) THICK
BLOCKBOARD OR PLYWOOD

50 x 25 mm (2 x 1 in)
BATTEN SCREWED
TO BOARD

BENCH TOP

FIGURE 1

Holes or openings can be cut by drilling a hole through the work-piece of a size through which the blade will just pass and in a position considered to be best suited, e.g. at the corner of an opening for a window. The blade is released from its fixing at the top of the saw frame. It is then threaded through the hole in the work-piece from below it, and refixed to the frame. Normal sawing can then proceed (*Fig. 2*). When the opening has been cut the blade is released and the work-piece is removed.

Mechanised fretsaws are also available which are operated either by a foot treadle or by an electric motor. These, apart from relieving the user of the man-power required to operate a hand saw, leave both hands free to manipulate the work-piece and also maintain a constant stroke movement of the blade in a truly vertical position. In all other respects the technique of using this type of saw is similar to the use of a hand saw.

The cutting table

Whilst fret-sawing larger sized sheets of timber can be done by resting the work-piece directly on a work bench, it is essential for most cutting to use a cutting table which will provide a firm support to the work-piece at the position in which the cut is being made.

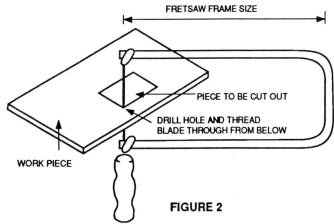

FRETSAW FRAME SIZE

PIECE TO BE CUT OUT

DRILL HOLE AND THREAD
BLADE THROUGH FROM BELOW

WORK PIECE

FIGURE 2

Various types of both wooden and metal cutting tables can be purchased. These are designed to be clamped to the work bench.

A suitable cutting table for use with the 'workmate' bench previously described can be easily made. It comprises a piece of timber in which a V-shaped notch is cut and to which a batten is fixed. It is secured to the bench by clamping the batten between the 'jaws' of the bench top (*Fig. 3*).

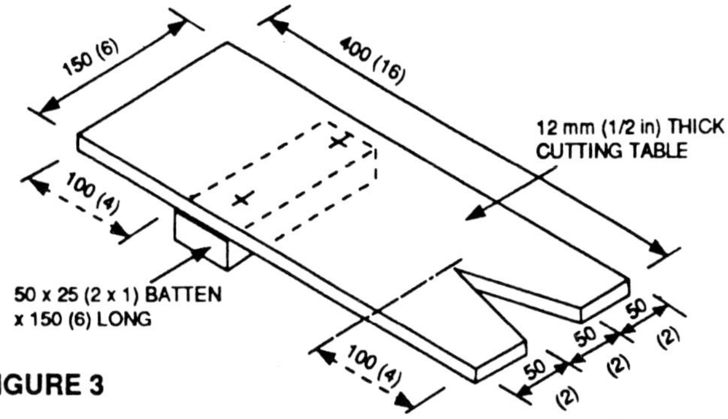

the maximum diameter required for making the toys described in this book. These drills are available in various sizes but a small to medium size is the more convenient to use for this kind of work.

There is no doubt that the power drill is superseding the hand drill. It is a particularly handy tool and when used in conjunction with a drill stand it can be used to drill holes which are vertically accurate.

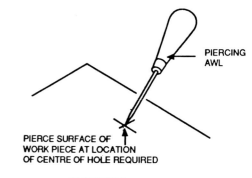

FIGURE 3

FIGURE 4

The piercing awl

This is a very simple tool which is nothing more than a handle on a sharply pointed piece of steel rod. It should be used to pierce the surface of a work-piece at a position where the piece is required to be drilled thus providing a positive location at which to present the tip of a drill bit when commencing to drill. This ensures that the hole to be drilled is accurately centred by minimising the possibility of the drill twist bit slipping away from its correct position at the start of the cut. (*Fig. 4*).

The drill and twist bits

A wheel-brace drill is a familiar hand tool which is adequate for drilling holes in timber using twist bits up to 6 mm ($\frac{1}{4}$ in) diameter, this being

For very small diameter holes such as those required to start pin-fixings (*see Section 2*) a mini drill of the type used by model-makers is more suitable than the larger standard size DIY power drills.

The twist bits to be used with the drill should always be sharp if good, clean holes are to be cut.

The pin hammer

This tool is a very light hammer used for hammering pins and small nails which a heavier hammer might easily bend. It is extensively used for many of the joints required in the making of the projects described in Section 3.

The trimming knife

This knife is a versatile tool which uses

disposable blades. These blades are razor sharp and they should be protected when not in use by pushing the blade into a piece of cork or india rubber – both to protect the cutting edge of the blade and for obvious safety reasons. The knife can be used for a number of tasks such as cutting parts out of the thin sheet materials, e.g. 1.5 mm ($\frac{1}{16}$ in) plywood or card; for forming chamfers (*see Section 2*); and general trimming (cleaning timber 'burrs' from rough saw cuts.

MATERIALS

Timber

The main timber used in the construction of the projects described in this book is plywood of 4 and 6 mm ($\frac{1}{8}$ and $\frac{1}{4}$ in) thicknesses.

When purchasing plywood look for a good quality sheet, free from open joints in the core material and with a surface veneer free from unsightly marks and with a pleasing colour and grain. Sheets with different coloured veneers (as a result of the use of different species of wood used in their manufacture) can be effectively used to provide colour contrast when finishing toys with a clear varnish.

Timber other than plywood is also required to a lesser extent. Despite the name, some hardwoods, especially mahogany, are easier to work than many softwoods. Also hardwoods present a better appearance when finished with a clear varnish.

Timber for fillets can be purchased in lengths of the finished sizes – 12 × 6 mm ($\frac{1}{2}$ × $\frac{1}{4}$ in) and 6 × 6 mm ($\frac{1}{4}$ × $\frac{1}{4}$ in). This obviates the task of cutting strips from 6 mm ($\frac{1}{4}$ in) thick sheet which, however, is a less expensive alternative.

Fixatives

Fret pins are very small nails of approximately 1 mm ($\frac{1}{32}$ in) diameter and are used to secure joints

where relatively thin (4 and 6 mm ($\frac{1}{8}$ and $\frac{1}{4}$ in)) sheets of timber are to be jointed together. They can be obtained in various lengths – 12, 15 and 18 mm ($\frac{1}{2}$, $\frac{5}{8}$ and $\frac{3}{4}$ in) – and are made of steel. Brass pins of smaller lengths – 6, 9 and 12 mm ($\frac{1}{4}$, $\frac{3}{8}$ and $\frac{1}{2}$ in) – are also obtainable.

Screws are used where a firmer joint is required and where timber sizes are sufficiently large to allow their use without splitting the timber. The screw most commonly used is the countersunk (c/s) head which, as its name implies, can be sunk level with, or below, the surface of the timber to be fixed.

Screws are normally made of steel or brass and are available in various sizes, classified by their gauge (the diameter of their shanks) and their overall lengths – the thinner the screw, the lower the gauge number (*Fig. 5*).

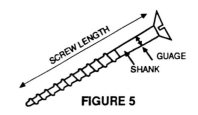

FIGURE 5

A useful gadget can easily be made to determine the diameter of hole required to be drilled to receive a screw (see '*Joints*' *in Section 2*). Take a piece of hardwood about 150 × 25 × 19 mm (6 × 1 × $\frac{3}{4}$ ins) and in it drill a series of holes varying in diameter from 1.5 to 6 mm ($\frac{1}{16}$ to $\frac{1}{4}$ in). Mark each hole to identify its diameter in metric or imperial as preferred (*Fig. 6*).

The diameter of hole required can be quickly determined by using this gadget to ascertain that hole into which the screw can be inserted when the hole of the next diameter down will not allow it to go in.

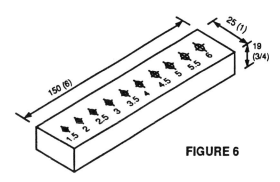

FIGURE 6

Adhesive

The glue recommended for general use is a white PVA quick-set adhesive which can be used on all woods. A light pressure will ensure a firm joint but where a stronger bond is required, a firmer pressure is required. The joints described in Section 2 are designed to maintain the necessary pressures by the use of fret pins or screw-fixings.

Surplus PVA adhesive should be wiped away from the surface of the timber with a damp cloth before it is allowed to dry, otherwise the timber will show the marks of the adhesive when clear varnish finishes are used. This is not so important when a colour paint finish is to be applied.

An impact adhesive also has its uses. The particular feature of this glue is that it is applied thinly to the two surfaces to be joined and allowed to dry. The surfaces are then brought together and they bond firmly and permanently on contact. A firm pressure is needed to bring about the bond. This adhesive can be used for securing stair treads and risers (*see 'Stairs' in Section 2*).

Sandpaper

A smooth finish must be given to the toys before they are painted or varnished. Because they are going to be handled by children it is particularly important that there are no splinters of wood and that all sharp corners are smoothly rounded.

Sandpaper, or glasspaper as it is sometimes known, is obtainable in various grades but a coarse grade is rarely required when plywoods and ready planed timbers are used. A medium grade is used to begin with and a fine grade is used to bring the surface to a final smooth finish.

An alternative to the common sandpaper is a paper coated with a high quality aluminium oxide abrasive which, although it is more expensive, is a longer lasting and more effective 'sandpaper'.

Finish coatings

The choice of how to finish a toy is a matter of personal preference. It is generally limited to using either paints, which provide a wide choice of colours, or varnish.

A good quality oil paint will provide a durable finish. It is normally applied in three or more coats, i.e. a primer, an undercoat and one or more finishing coats. There are new paint products on the market which claim to do away with the need for priming and undercoats but the author cannot recommend their use until they have been proved as suitable finishes for childrens' toys. One real advantage of using a paint finish is that it can cover any blemishes such as badly fitted joints which have been made good with a filler.

Varnishes can be obtained either clear or incorporating a stain. Clear varnish can produce either a matt, a semi–gloss (satin or egg-shell), or a full-gloss finish. Clear varnishes can be used to effect when woods of different colours have been used in a toy's construction. Alternatively, wood stains can be used to provide colour contrast to parts of the toy (e.g. the roofs and windows) before a final finish of clear varnish is applied. It might be said that the disadvantage of using varnish is that the toy must be well finished – 'mistakes' in construction cannot be hidden, they might even be highlighted.

Whichever finish is used, paint or varnish, it must be safe for children to handle. In this respect it must not contain elements which, if present in relatively large quantities, can be harmful – lead in particular.

There is a third optional finish, namely, patterned paper. These papers are obtainable in a variety of effects such as brick, slate, stone, tiles and parquet flooring, as well as different wallpaper designs. They are all made to suit a toy made to a scale of approximately 1:12. The papers are recommended for fixing with a cellulose adhesive like those used for hanging normal wallpapers, but it is considered that a better and more durable finish is achieved if they are fixed with a PVA adhesive as described earlier. Fixing in this manner may take a little more effort but the paper finish can then be given a coat of clear varnish to make it yet more resistant to wear and tear.

SECTION 2

CONSTRUCTION DETAILS

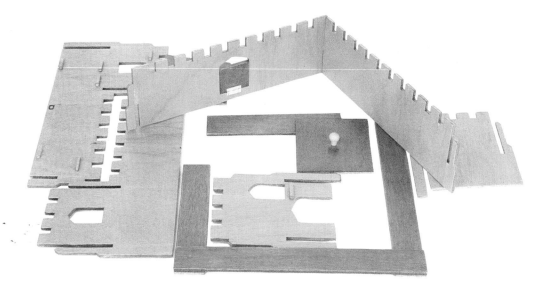

T he information contained in this section is intended to provide helpful advice on various construction requirements for making the toys described in Section 3. From time to time reference to this section will be made within the Construction Details included with each of the toy-making projects, therefore a perusal of the information to familiarise the reader with its contents should prove to be helpful. Once a start is made with the construction of the toys it will probably be necessary to refer back to this section for amplification of the instructions given.

Marking Out

Before any work can commence, the shapes of the components to be made, as illustrated and dimensioned on the plans, must be marked out on the surface of the timber (of the requisite thickness) from which they are to be cut. This process should be carried out using a soft pencil (H or HB), a measuring tape and/or rule, a straight edge (to draw straight lines) and a try square (to mark out right angles). In addition a compass is needed to mark out circles, or segments of circles, of given radii.

It is recommended that initially only the cut-lines (those lines along which a piece is to be cut) should be marked out thus allowing the piece to be cut out and sanded smooth before other marking (to locate the positions of fillets and other adjoining components) is completed.

Joints

The jointing of relatively thin sheets of timber, such as plywood, is achieved by the use of fret pins in conjunction with a PVA adhesive. The prime purpose of the pins is to maintain a close contact with, and pressure on, the surfaces to be joined until such time as the adhesive has achieved a firm bond.

The location of fixing pins in the timber through which they are to pass must always a be pre-drilled with holes of the same diameter as the gauge of the pins, or marginally less. This ensures that the pins will be accurately positioned and is particularly necessary when they are to be hammered into the edge of a thin piece of timber such as plywood. After applying glue to the contact surfaces of the joint the timbers can be brought together in their correct jointed-position and the pins carefully hammered 'home'. The joint should then be left until the glue has achieved its full bond.

One method of obtaining a satisfactory joint between two pieces of plywood meeting at a 90° angle is as follows (Fig. 7):

i.   Place sheet A on a flat bench surface with the edge opposite to that to be jointed hard

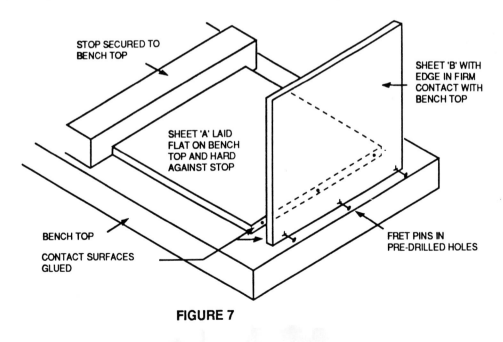

STOP SECURED TO BENCH TOP

SHEET 'B' WITH EDGE IN FIRM CONTACT WITH BENCH TOP

SHEET 'A' LAID FLAT ON BENCH TOP AND HARD AGAINST STOP

BENCH TOP

CONTACT SURFACES GLUED

FRET PINS IN PRE-DRILLED HOLES

FIGURE 7

against a stop secured to the bench.

ii.   Pre-drill sheet B in the required pin fixing positions and hammer pins into the holes so that their points barely protrude.

iii. Apply adhesive to the contact surface of the joint.

iv.   Place sheet B in its position against sheet A and with its edge firmly against the bench top and hammer 'home' the pins.

v.   Ensure that the joint is square and allow it to set firm.

This method facilitates the handling of the sheets of timber and ensures that the joint edges are properly aligned.

The joint between thin sheets can be further stiffened by fixing a fillet (a strip of wood) into the angle of the joint. Such a fillet can also help to pre–locate the pieces to be jointed. The fillet is fixed to the sheet through which the fixing pins are to pass by glueing and pinning. It is located with an edge against the required line of the face of the sheet to which the other one is to be fixed (*Figure 8*).

The jointing of a thin sheet to a thicker piece of timber, or of larger sizes of timber, one to another, is achieved by the use of screws in conjunction with PVA adhesive. In this case, the screws not only maintain a firmer pressure between the glued surfaces whilst the bond is achieved, but they also provide additional fixing stability.

As explained previously, always pre–drill the positions of the screws, in the timber through which they are to pass, with holes of a diameter marginally larger than the gauge of the screws to be used (*see 'Fixatives' in Section 1*). If counter-sunk screws are to be used the tops of the holes should also be counter–sunk to receive the screw heads. Additionally with screw–fixings it is recommended that the location into which the screw is to be driven should be pre–drilled with a hole of a diameter somewhat less than the screw gauge, say about 1.5 mm ($\frac{1}{16}$ in) depending on the hardness of the wood – the harder the wood, the larger the hole diameter into which the screw is to be driven, but it must never be as large a diameter as the screw gauge, for the obvious reason that the screw would not achieve a hold in such an out–sized hole.

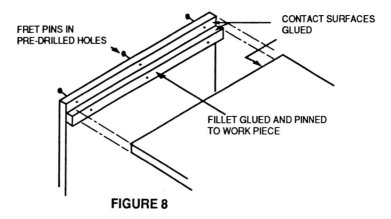

FRET PINS IN
PRE-DRILLED HOLES

CONTACT SURFACES
GLUED

FILLET GLUED AND PINNED
TO WORK PIECE

FIGURE 8

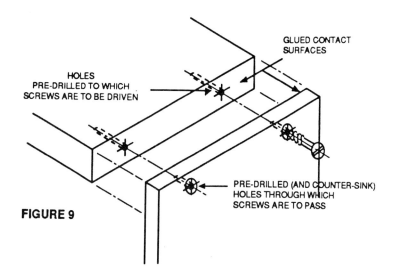

FIGURE 9

The procedure for constructing a screwed joint is as follows (*Fig. 9*):

 i. Pre-drill (and counter-sink if necessary) holes in the required positions in the piece through which the screws are to pass.

 ii. With the work-pieces held together in the position in which they are to be joined, insert a screw in each hole and drive each in just sufficiently to mark the surface of the wood into which they will be driven.

 iii. At each of these marks pre-drill a hole of a diameter slightly smaller than the screw gauge (as previously explained) and of a depth about equal to that which the screw is likely to reach.

 iv. Apply adhesive to the contact surface of the joint.

 v. Put together the work-pieces in their correct jointed position and drive 'home' the screws.

 vi. Allow the joint to set firm.

Mitres and Chamfers

The joints previously described have been simple butt joints where one edge of the two jointed pieces is exposed to its end grain. In some circumstances it is not acceptable to have such an exposed edge and it is, therefore, necessary to form a mitred cut where the ends (or edges) of two pieces meet and join. Where the joint angle is to be 90° each mitre needs to be cut at a 45° angle so that they form a 90° return when joined (*Fig. 10*).

Mitred joints are required on the cornices and architraves described on some of the Section 3

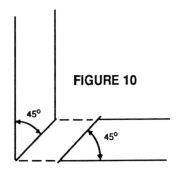

FIGURE 10

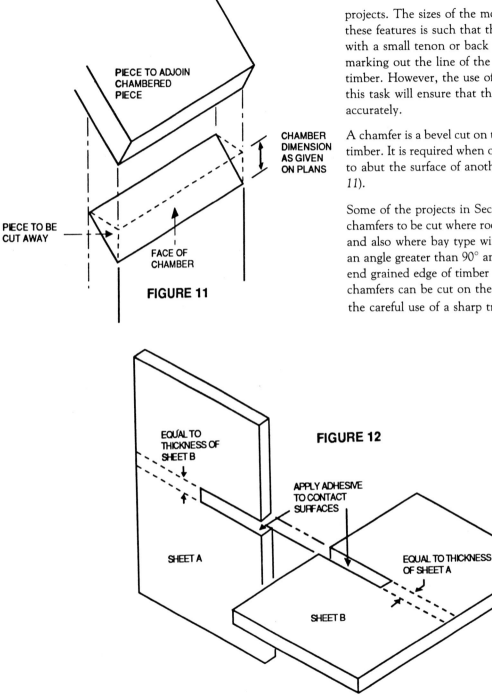

PIECE TO ADJOIN
CHAMBERED
PIECE

CHAMBER
DIMENSION
AS GIVEN
ON PLANS

PIECE TO BE
CUT AWAY

FACE OF
CHAMBER

FIGURE 11

projects. The sizes of the mouldings used for these features is such that the mitres can be cut with a small tenon or back saw after carefully marking out the line of the 45° cut on the timber. However, the use of a mitre block for this task will ensure that the mitres are cut accurately.

A chamfer is a bevel cut on the edge of a piece of timber. It is required when one piece of timber is to abut the surface of another at an angel (*Fig. 11*).

Some of the projects in Section 3 require chamfers to be cut where roofs abut one another and also where bay type windows are joined at an angle greater than 90° and where an exposed end grained edge of timber is undesirable. Such chamfers can be cut on the edge of plywood by the careful use of a sharp trimming knife, after

EQUAL TO
THICKNESS OF
SHEET B

FIGURE 12

APPLY ADHESIVE
TO CONTACT
SURFACES

SHEET A

EQUAL TO THICKNESS
OF SHEET A

SHEET B

marking out the line to which the chamfer is to be cut. This line is to be set back from the edge of the work-piece by the dimension given on the plans for the particular chamfer.

Interlocking Joint

This is a useful type of joint which can be used to join two pieces of sheet, such as plywod, when their planes are to be at 90° to one another. It is achieved by cutting a slot into each of the two pieces along the positions at which they are to be joined and of a width equal to the thickness of the pieces. The joint is completed by applying adhesive to the contact surfaces and sliding each piece together along the length of the slots (*Fig. 12*).

This type of joint is used on some of the projects described in Section 3.

Windows

The method adapted for making windows for the Section 3 projects is as follows (*Fig. 13*):

i. Having marked out and cut out the walls, cut out the windows to form their openings as described in Section 1 (use of fret-saw) and retain the pieces cut out. When originally marking out the window openings it is recommended that each window piece be identified in some way, e.g. by its wall identification, so that it can be replaced in the same opening from which it was cut.

ii. Mark out on the window pieces the outline of the fenestration (frames) and cut out the panes in a similar manner to that required to cut out other openings.

iii. Finish each window by sand-papering until

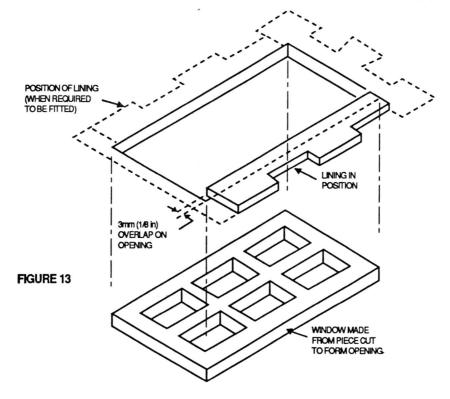

POSITION OF LINING (WHEN REQUIRED TO BE FITTED)

LINING IN POSITION

3mm (1/8 in) OVERLAP ON OPENING

FIGURE 13

WINDOW MADE FROM PIECE CUT TO FORM OPENING.

smooth. Paint or stain as desired, and allow to dry.

iv. On some projects the windows can now be completed by simply applying PVA adhesive around their edges and reinserting them into the openings from which they were originally cut, wiping clean any surplus

adhesive from around them, and leaving to allow the adhesive to achieve its bond.

v. On other projects a lining is to be fixed around the window opening in such a way as to provide a 3 mm ($\frac{1}{8}$ in) overlap around the opening. This creates a rebate into which the window will be seated.

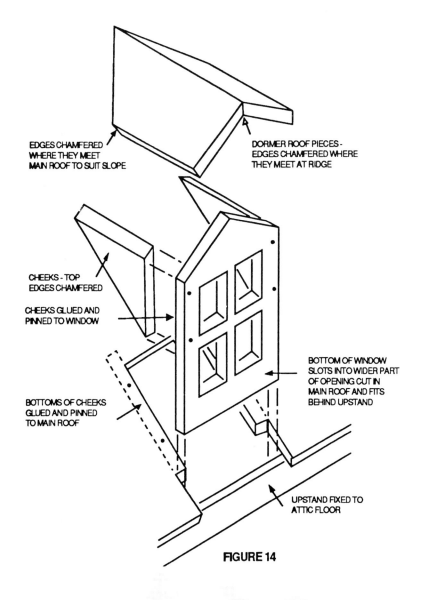

EDGES CHAMFERED WHERE THEY MEET MAIN ROOF TO SUIT SLOPE

DORMER ROOF PIECES - EDGES CHAMFERED WHERE THEY MEET AT RIDGE

CHEEKS - TOP EDGES CHAMFERED

CHEEKS GLUED AND PINNED TO WINDOW

BOTTOM OF WINDOW SLOTS INTO WIDER PART OF OPENING CUT IN MAIN ROOF AND FITS BEHIND UPSTAND

BOTTOMS OF CHEEKS GLUED AND PINNED TO MAIN ROOF

UPSTAND FIXED TO ATTIC FLOOR

FIGURE 14

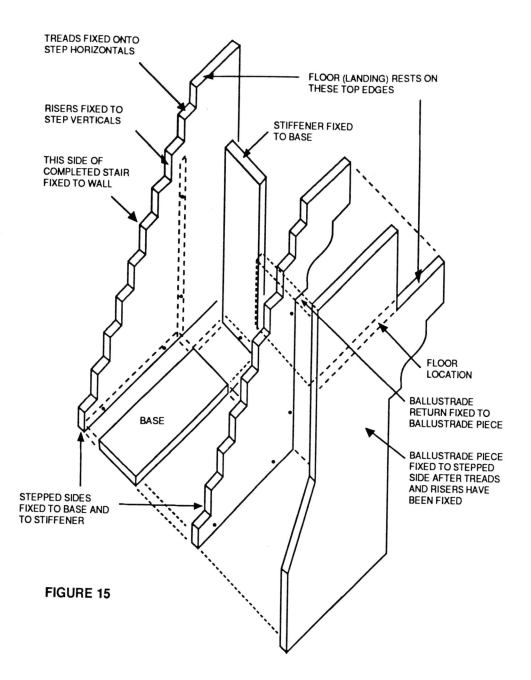

TREADS FIXED ONTO
STEP HORIZONTALS

FLOOR (LANDING) RESTS ON
THESE TOP EDGES

RISERS FIXED TO
STEP VERTICALS

STIFFENER FIXED
TO BASE

THIS SIDE OF
COMPLETED STAIR
FIXED TO WALL

FLOOR
LOCATION

BASE

BALLUSTRADE
RETURN FIXED TO
BALLUSTRADE PIECE

BALLUSTRADE PIECE
FIXED TO STEPPED
SIDE AFTER TREADS
AND RISERS HAVE
BEEN FIXED

STEPPED SIDES
FIXED TO BASE AND
TO STIFFENER

FIGURE 15

vi. Complete the windows as before by applying adhesive around the rebate formed by the action of instruction v. (above) and re-insert the windows into the openings from which they were originally cut, wiping clean any surplus adhesive, leave to allow the adhesive to achieve its bond.

The dormer windows fitted to the Georgian Dolls' House are each made up from five pieces – the window (frame), a pair of cheeks and a pair of roofs. The cheeks are chamfered at their top edge and are glued and pinned to the back of the window. The roofs are chamfered where they meet at the ridge and also where they meet the slope of the main roof to receive them (*Fig. 14*).

The sequence of assembly of the dormer windows is described in the Construction Details for the Georgian Dolls' House project.

Stairs

The method adapted for making stairs for the Section 3 projects is one that allows all the pieces to be cut out of plywood of 4 and 6 mm ($\frac{1}{8}$ and $\frac{1}{4}$ in) thicknesses. It also produces a stair of a pleasing and realistic appearance.

A 'framework' is formed of two stepped pieces fixed to a base and to a vertical stiffener which also closes the back of the stair (*Fig. 15*). To this 'framework' are fixed the treads and risers which can be glued using an impact adhesive or they can be glued and pinned using PVA adhesive with 6 mm ($\frac{1}{4}$ in) fret pins. It is more convenient to commence with the fixing of the bottom riser, then the bottom tread, followed by the next riser and tread, and so on until the top is reached.

The exposed edges of the treads and risers on one side are covered when that side is fixed against a wall. On the other side they are covered by a piece which also forms the balustrade.

Further embellishments can be added to improve the appearance of the stair if desired, but they are not included in the instructions for making the Section 3 Dolls' House projects. A newel post can be fixed to the bottom of the piece forming the balustrade and a hand-rail capping can be fixed to the top of the balustrades – the newel using a short length of 9 × 9 mm ($\frac{3}{8}$ × ($\frac{3}{8}$ in) timber and the capping using strips of 9 × 4 mm ($\frac{3}{8}$ × $\frac{1}{8}$ in) timber.

The floor to which the stair gives access is shaped with a cut-out into which the stair fits with the landing resting on the extensions of the two stepped pieces.

The sequence of assembly of the stairs is described in the project Construction Details. The Tudor Dolls' House has a stair which is constructed in two flights but the method of construction is similar to that for a straight-flight stair.

Attic Ladder

A ladder can be fitted to give access to the trap door in the Attic floor of some of the dolls' houses. It is easily constructed with two sides cut from 6 mm ($\frac{1}{4}$ in) plywood shaped to allow them to be fixed to a wall. Each side is drilled to receive the ladder rungs. The most suitable way in which to ensure that the holes are drilled exactly opposite each other is to tape each completed side together with an adhesive tape and after marking the position of the rungs on the one side, drill holes of the requisite diameter through the two pieces (*Fig. 16*).

After the holes have been drilled, secure a precut length of dowel into each hole on one side and then secure the other side onto the other ends of the dowels to complete the ladder (*Fig. 17*).

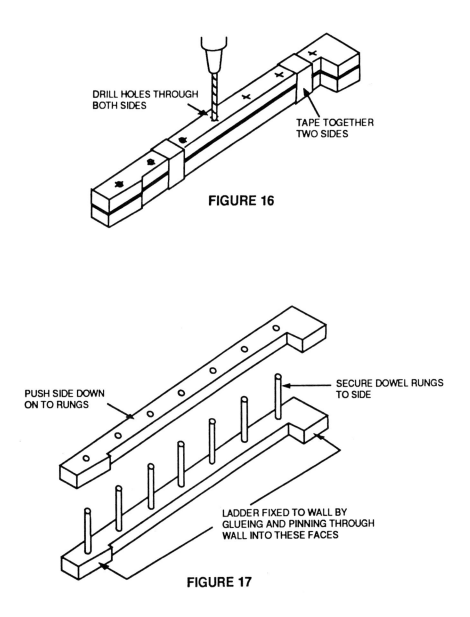

DRILL HOLES THROUGH
BOTH SIDES

TAPE TOGETHER
TWO SIDES

FIGURE 16

PUSH SIDE DOWN
ON TO RUNGS

SECURE DOWEL RUNGS
TO SIDE

LADDER FIXED TO WALL BY
GLUEING AND PINNING THROUGH
WALL INTO THESE FACES

FIGURE 17

SECTION 3

TOY-MAKING PROJECTS

Before you begin to make a start with the construction of the projects described in this section it is recommended that due notice be taken of the following explanatory notes.

The projects vary in degrees of intricacy rather than difficulty and careful study of the instructions and plans will clarify the processes of construction required.

The basic material used is plywood of different thicknesses, generally 4 mm ($\frac{1}{8}$ in) and 6 mm ($\frac{1}{4}$ in) thick. The actual thickness of plywood can vary from its nominal thickness. Any such variation should be ascertained and, if necessary, corresponding adjustments made to the dimensions as given on the plans.

It is important to note the direction from which components are viewed and represented on the plans. Failure to do so may result in parts being cut out the opposite way round to that which they should be.

Dimensions are given in both metric (millimetres) and imperial (inches). The metric dimension is given first with its imperial equivalent given in brackets either after or below the metric. The imperial dimension is not necessarily an exact conversion of its relative metric. This does not in any way affect the viability of the plans as long as the dimensions are not mixed – stick with either the metric or with the imperial.

The Cutting List included with the instructions for each projects is an aid which describes the quantity of different sizes of timber required to make the toy. For example, from a sheet of a given size and thickness of plywood given in the list, all the components required to be cut from plywood of that thickness can be obtained for that particular project.

The construction details must be read in conjunction with the plans. Cultivate the practice of referring to a component as illustrated on the plans when it is specifically mentioned in the Details. This practice will become second nature as experience is gained. Time spent studying the Construction Details in conjunction with the plans to ensure that the instructions are fully understood before commencing construction will help to prevent mistakes being made as the work proceeds.

Although not specifically mentioned in the Construction Details all component parts should be sanded and smoothed ready to receive the applied finishes *before* they are assembled. Also, all holes for screw-and pin-fixings should be pre-drilled *before* the assembly of component parts takes place. It will be much easier to carry out these tasks at this early stage rather than during or after assembly.

Occasionally reference is made in the Construction Details to suitable times to apply the finish (paint, varnish, etc.) to component parts before proceeding further, because of the difficulty of applying the finish to the toy when assembly is completed. Thought should be given at all stages of construction to the convenience of applying the internal finishes, especially if wallpaper is to be used for finishing the rooms in the Dolls' House.

Symbols used on the plans

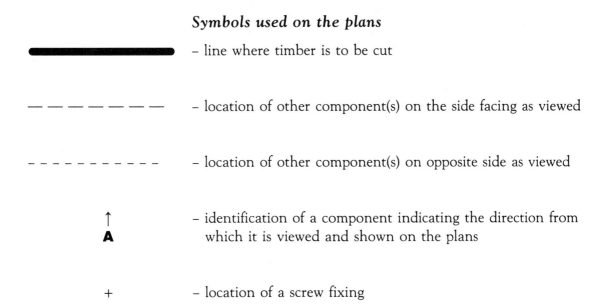

– line where timber is to be cut

– location of other component(s) on the side facing as viewed

– location of other component(s) on opposite side as viewed

– identification of a component indicating the direction from which it is viewed and shown on the plans

– location of a screw fixing

Unless otherwise indicated, the thickness of all components illustrated on the plans is 6 mm ($\frac{1}{4}$ in)

PROJECT 1

CASTLE 'FLAT-PACK'

This little toy is a helpful exercise in using the fret–saw for cutting plywood. It is designed so that the pieces slot together and therefore it can be assembled and taken apart by children as part of the play function.

As a result of this form of construction any pinning and glueing is limited to the fixing of fillets as floor/rampart/roof supports.

CUTTING LIST

900 × 900 × 6 mm (36 × 24 × ¼ in)   plywood

6 × 6 × 682 mm (¼ in × ¼ in × 26½ in)   timber fillet

6 mm (¼ in) diameter × 36 mm (1½ in) timber dowel

ANCILLARIES

1 No. 25 mm (1 in) brass hinge

1 No. small knob

CONSTRUCTION DETAILS

1. Mark and cut out all the components, ie the Castle and Tower floors; the Tower roof; sides A, B, C, D, E and F; and ramparts G, H, J and K.

2. Cut out the opening for the drawbridge from side A and use the piece cut out to make the drawbridge.

3. Fix 4 No. 25 mm (1 in) long fillets to side A to support ramparts G and H and the Castle floor. Fix the hinge to the drawbridge and fix it into the opening in side A to open outwards.

4. Fix 2 No. 25 mm (1 in) long fillets to side B to support the Castle floor.

5. Fix 3 No. 25 mm (1 in) long fillets to side C to support the Castle floor and the Tower roof.

6. Fix 4 No. 25 mm (1 in) long and one 116 mm (4¼ in) long fillets to side D to support the Castle and Tower floors, the Tower roof and rampart H.

7. Fix 2 No. 25 mm (1 in) long and one 116 mm (4¼ ins) long fillets to side E to support the Tower floor and roof, and rampart G.

8. Fix 2 No. 25 mm (1 in) long fillets to side F to support the Tower roof and rampart J.

9. Drill one 6 mm (¼ in) diameter hole at one end of rampart G and fix a 12 mm (½ in) long fillet at the other end and to the underside of this rampart, taking care to ensure the correct relative positions of the hole and fillet.

10. Drill 2 No. 6 mm (¼ in) diameter holes in rampart H, one at each end.

11. Drill one 6 mm (¼ in) diameter hole at one end of rampart J and fix into it a 6 mm (¼ in) diameter dowel to project 6 mm (¼ in) below the underside. Fix a 12 mm (½ in) long fillet at the other end and to the underside of this rampart taking care to ensure the correct relative positions of the dowel and fillet.

12. Drill 2 No. 6 mm (¼ in) diameter holes in rampart K (one at each end) and fix into each hole a 6 mm (¼ in) diameter dowel to project 6 mm (¼ in) below the underside.

13. Fix a small knob to the top surface of the Tower roof to facilitate the lifting of the roof.

14. Finish all components with a paint or stain and varnish finish, and identify each component part with its correct identification letter to facilitate assembly of the completed toy.

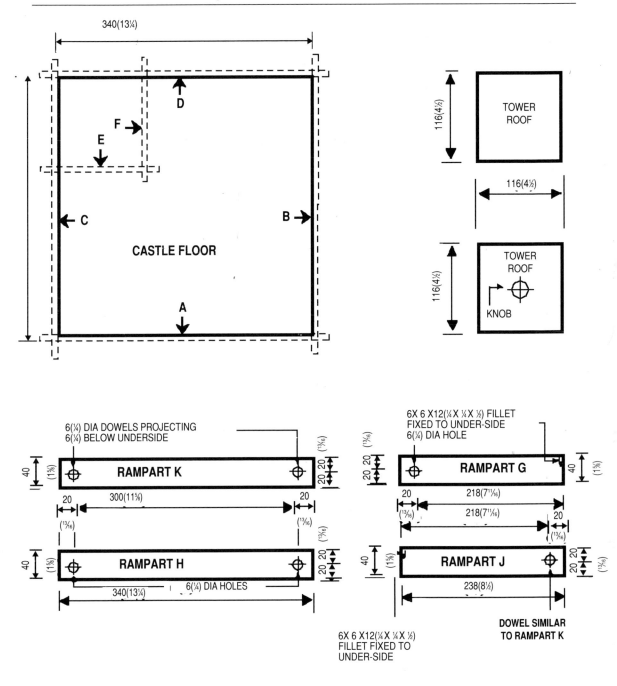

340(13¼)

CASTLE FLOOR

D

F

E

C

B

A

116(4½)

TOWER ROOF

116(4½)

116(4½)

TOWER ROOF

KNOB

6(¼) DIA DOWELS PROJECTING
6(¼) BELOW UNDERSIDE

RAMPART K

40 (1⅝)

20 20 (¹³⁄₁₆)

20

300(11⅝)

20

6X 6 X12(¼ X ¼ X ½) FILLET
FIXED TO UNDER-SIDE
6(¼) DIA HOLE

(¹³⁄₁₆)

20 20

RAMPART G

40 (1⅝)

20

218(7¹¹⁄₁₆)

(¹³⁄₁₆)

(¹³⁄₁₆)

RAMPART H

40 (1⅝)

20 20 (¹³⁄₁₆)

340(13¼)

6(¼) DIA HOLES

218(7¹¹⁄₁₆)

20

(¹³⁄₁₆)

40 (1⅝)

RAMPART J

20 20 (¹³⁄₁₆)

238(8½)

6X 6 X12(¼ X ¼ X ½)
FILLET FIXED TO
UNDER-SIDE

**DOWEL SIMILAR
TO RAMPART K**

CASTLE 'FLAT PACK'

SHEET 1

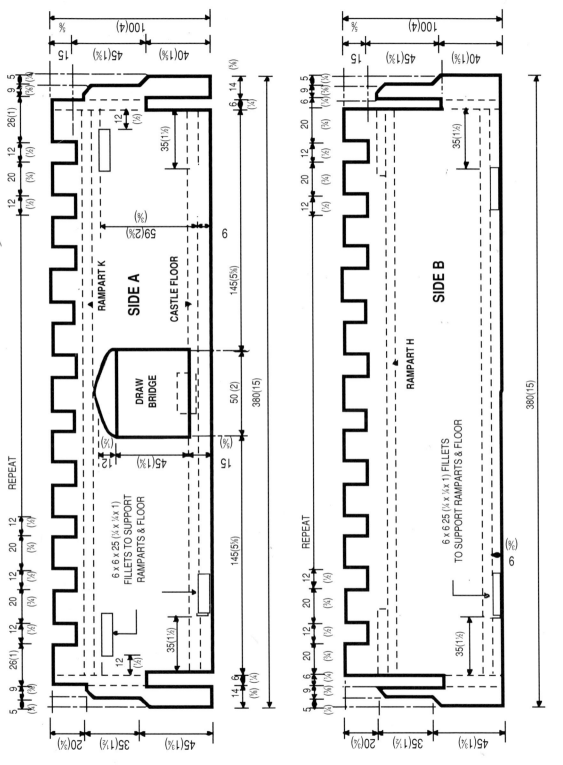

CASTLE 'FLAT-PACK'

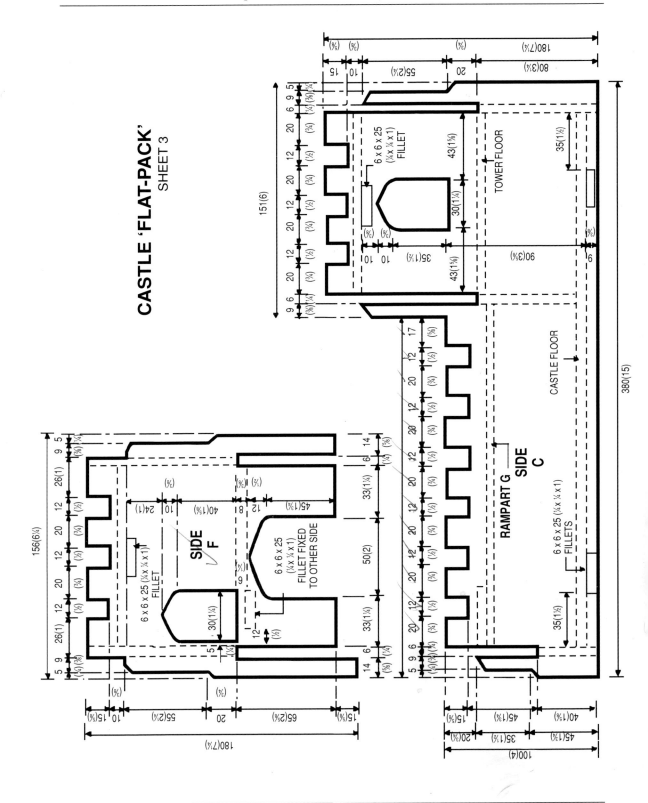

CASTLE 'FLAT-PACK' SHEET 3

CASTLE 'FLAT-PACK'

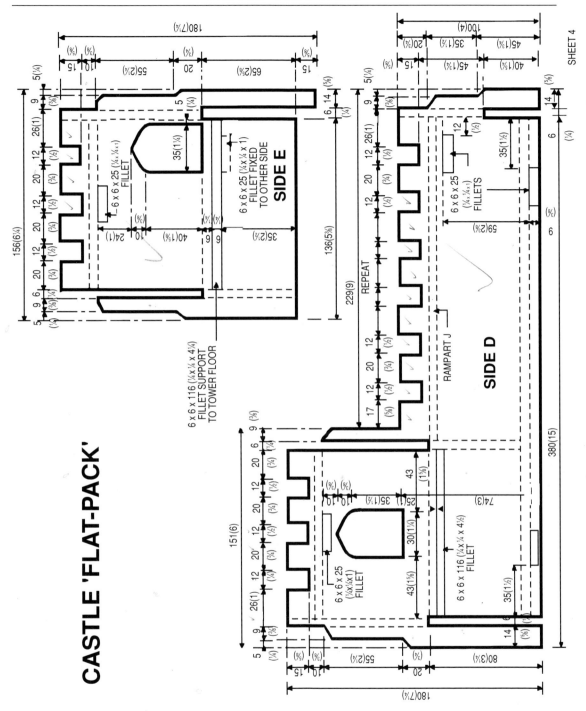

SHEET 4

SIDE E

SIDE D

REPEAT

RAMPART J

6 x 6 x 25 (¼ x ¼ x 1) FILLET

6 x 6 x 25 (¼ x ¼ x 1) FILLET FIXED TO OTHER SIDE

6 x 6 x 116 (¼ x ¼ x 4¼) FILLET SUPPORT TO TOWER FLOOR

6 x 6 x 25 (¼ x ¼ x 1) FILLETS

6 x 6 x 116 (¼ x ¼ x 4½) FILLET

6 x 6 x 25 (¼ x ¼ x 1) FILLET

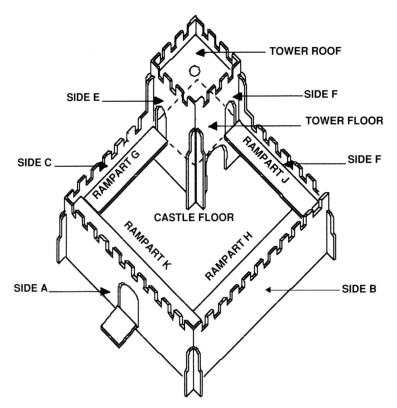

TOWER ROOF

SIDE E

SIDE F

TOWER FLOOR

SIDE C

SIDE F

RAMPART G

RAMPART J

CASTLE FLOOR

RAMPART K

RAMPART H

SIDE A

SIDE B

ASSEMBLY SEQUENCE

1. SLOT TOGETHER SIDES A, B, C & D

2. INSERT CASTLE FLOOR

3. SLOT TOGETHER SIDE E TO SIDE C

4. SLIDE IN TOWER FLOOR

5. SLOT TOGETHER SIDE F TO SIDES D & E

6. INSERT TOWER ROOF

7. INSERT RAMPARTS G & H

8. INSERT RAMPARTS J & K LOCATING STUDS INTO HOLES IN G & H

CASTLE 'FLAT-PACK'

SHEET 5

PROJECT 2

'COTTAGE' DOLLS HOUSE

T he traditional Scottish two room cottage with its 'crow-stepped' gables provides the model for this basic but attractive dolls' house.

Its construction incorporates most of the details described in Section 2 with the exception of a stair and accordingly it is a useful 'starter' for the beginner.

The finished toy is also well suited as a younger child's first dolls' house with its removable roof providing easy access to the rooms inside.

CUTTING LIST

532 × 300 × 12 mm (21 × 12 × ½ in)　　　plywood
1200 × 750 × 6 mm (48 × 30 × ¼ in)　　　plywood
300 × 150 × 4 mm (12 × 6 × ⅛ ins)　　　plywood
420 × 100 × 18 mm (16½ × 4 × ¾ in)　　timber
6 × 6 × 910 mm (¼ × ¼ × 36 in)　　　timber fillet
6 mm (¼ in) diameter × 6 mm (¼ in)　　timber dowel

ANCILLARIES

1 pair 25 mm (1 in) brass hinges

1 pair small knobs

CONSTRUCTION DETAILS

1. Mark and cut out the components for the base and walls A, B, C, D, E, F and G.

2. Complete the cutting of the windows, door and fanlight, using the pieces cut from walls A and B to form their openings (*as described in Section 2*). Stain or paint these items and put them aside to dry.

3. Cut from 4 mm (⅛ in) thick plywood the pieces to form the window linings and glue and pin them around the sides and tops of the window openings in walls A and B so that they overlap the openings 2 mm (⅛ in). Note that a triangular shaped piece of lining is fixed to the tops of the windows on the front wall A so that it aligns with the triangular shaped projection above each window opening.

4. Cut from 6 mm (¼ in) thick plywood the pieces to form the window sills and glue and pin them to the bottoms of the window openings in walls A and B so that they overlap the openings 2 mm (⅛ in).

5. Cut from 4 mm (⅛ in) thick plywood the pieces to form the door/farlight facings and glue and pin them around the doorway opening in wall A so that they overlap the openings 2 mm (⅛ in).

6. Glue the windows and fanlight into the openings from which they were originally cut in walls A and B so that they are seated in the rebates formed by the linings and facings previously fixed around the openings.

7. Fix a door knob (made as described in the details of Project 10 – the Corner Shop) to the front of the door leaf. Fix one pair of 25 mm (1 in) hinges to the back of the door and then locate it in its opening in wall A and secure it by fixing the hinges to the side of the opening so that it opens inwards with the stops formed by the overlap of the facings previously fixed around the opening.

8. Cut from the requisite thicknesses of timber the two sets of parts to form the chimney stacks and fireplaces and fix them to each gable wall C and D as follows:

i.　Glue and pin the mantlepiece to the top of the fireplace piece.

ii.　Glue and pin the assembly of fireplace and mantlepiece in its correct position on the inside of the gable wall ensuring that the bottom of the fire-place is 12 mm (½ in) above the bottom of the wall to provide clearance for the 12 mm (½ in) thick base to be fixed to the wall.

iii. Glue and pin the chimney stack to the wall so that its bottom edge is hard against the mantlepiece and its top is aligned with the chimney projection at the top of the wall, and flush with its top edge.

iv.　Repeat the instructions to fix the chimney/fireplace to the other gable wall.

9. Glue and pin the two lengths of 6 × 6 mm (¼ × ¼ in) fillet to the inside of each of the gable walls C and D in the positions indicated on the plans. These will provide a seating for the roofs.

10. Glue and screw wall A to the base using 4 No $\frac{5}{8}$ in × 4 countersunk (c/s) screws.

11. Glue and screw wall B to the base using 4 No $\frac{5}{8}$ in × 4 c/s screws.

12. Glue and screw gable wall C to the base using 2 No $\frac{5}{8}$ in × 4 c/s screws and pin through C into the ends of walls A and B.

13. Glue and screw gable wall D to the base using 2 No $\frac{5}{8}$ in × 4 c/s screws and pin through D into the ends of walls A and B.

14. Glue and insert wall E into its position and secure it by pinning through walls A and B into its ends.

15. Secure wall F into its position as instruction 14 for wall E.

16. Glue and insert wall G into its position and secure it by pinning through walls E and F into its ends.

This is an opportune time to apply the desired finish to the inside of the house, especially if the walls are to be papered.

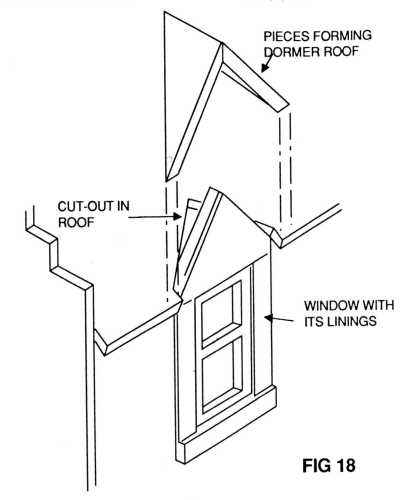

PIECES FORMING DORMER ROOF

CUT-OUT IN ROOF

WINDOW WITH ITS LININGS

FIG 18

17. Mark and cut out the fixed roof component and cut the two chamfers on its underside at the notches formed to fit around the chimneys.

18. Glue and pin the length of 6 × 6 mm ($\frac{1}{4}$ × $\frac{1}{4}$ in) fillet to the underside of the fixed roof along its top edge.

19. Glue and locate the fixed roof in its position properly seated on the fillets fixed to the gable walls C and D and with the triangular shaped projections above the wall A windows located within the cut–outs in the roof. Ensure that the top edge of the roof is located such that the removable roof, when seated its position (*see instruction 22*) will also fit neatly against this edge of the fixed roof. When satisfied, pin through gable walls C and D into the edges of the roof to secure it.

20. Cut out the pieces to form the two sets of dormer roofs and cut the chamfers on their undersides. Check and adjust them for a proper fit to each other and to the triangular-shaped projections above the wall A windows and to the fixed roof. When satisfied, glue and pin them into position (*Fig. 18*).

21. Mark and cut out the removable roof component and cut the two chamfers on its underside at the notches formed to fit around the chimneys.

22. Glue and pin the two lengths of 6 × 6 mm ($\frac{1}{4}$ × $\frac{1}{4}$ in) fillet to the underside of the removable roof after ensuring that they are positioned so as to properly locate this roof when it is seated in its required location on the fillets fixed to gable walls C and D. Complete this roof by fixing two small knobs to its top surface to facilitate its lifting.

23. Complete the chimneys by cutting out the two capping pieces and fixing them to the tops of the stacks.

24. Apply the final finishes of paint or varnish to the house to complete it. The toy shown in the photograph has had its chimney stacks finished with a masonry patterned paper. If such a finish is required it is recommended that it be applied after completion of instruction 8.

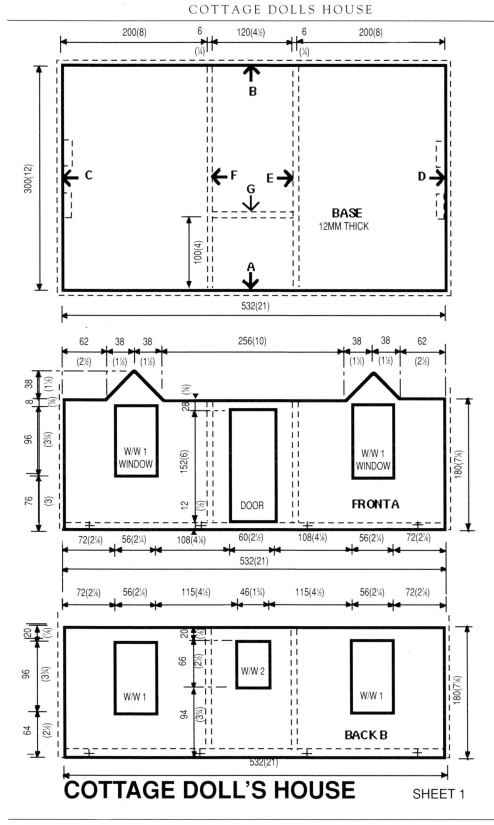

COTTAGE DOLL'S HOUSE

SHEET 1

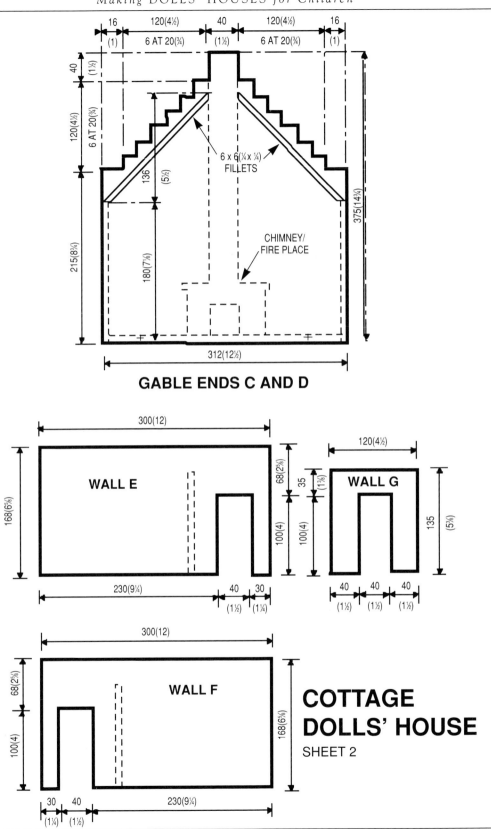

GABLE ENDS C AND D

WALL E

WALL G

WALL F

COTTAGE DOLLS' HOUSE
SHEET 2

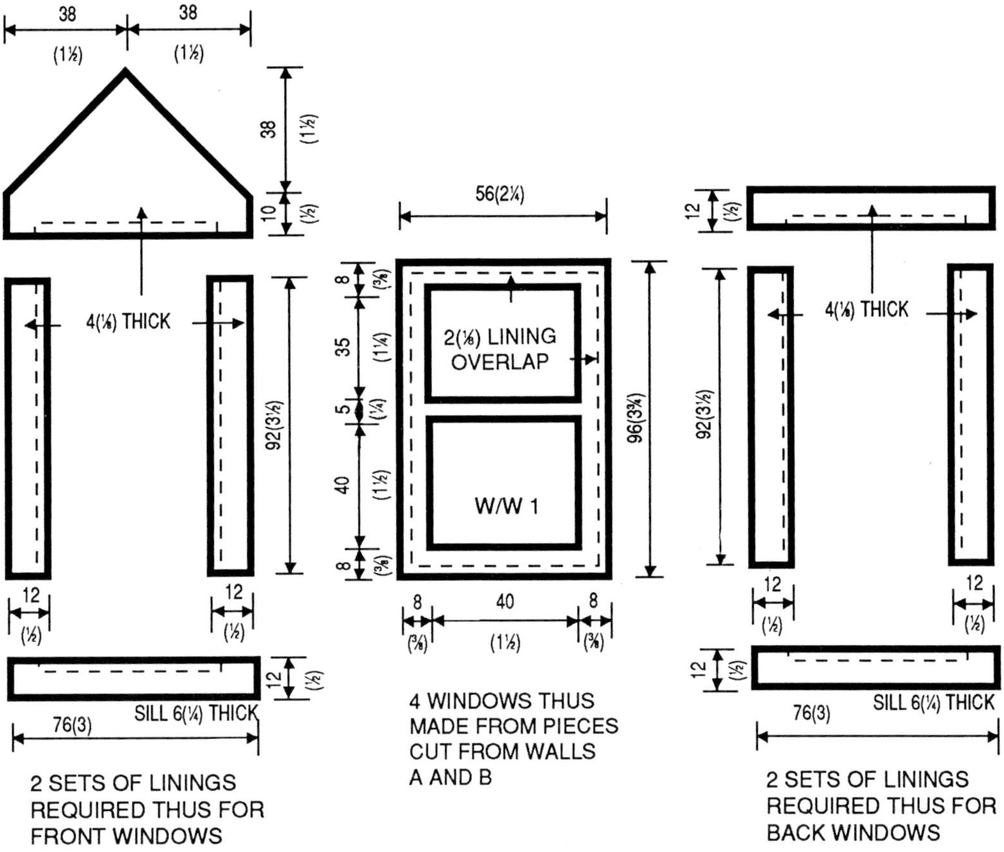
38
(1½)
38
(1½)
38
(1½)
10
(½)
4(⅛) THICK
92(3½)
12
(½)
12
(½)
12
(½)
SILL 6(¼) THICK
76(3)
2 SETS OF LININGS
REQUIRED THUS FOR
FRONT WINDOWS
56(2¼)
8
(⅜)
35
(1¼)
5
(¼)
40
(1½)
8
(⅜)
2(⅛) LINING
OVERLAP
W/W 1
96(3¾)
8
40
8
(⅜)
(1½)
(⅜)
4 WINDOWS THUS
MADE FROM PIECES
CUT FROM WALLS
A AND B
12
(½)
4(⅛) THICK
92(3½)
12
(½)
12
(½)
12
(½)
SILL 6(¼) THICK
76(3)
2 SETS OF LININGS
REQUIRED THUS FOR
BACK WINDOWS

WINDOWS TYPE W/W1

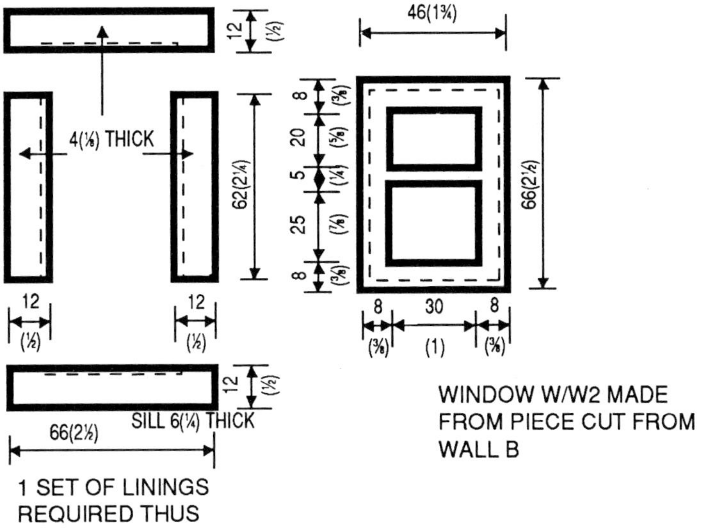
12
(½)
4(⅛) THICK
62(2¼)
12
(½)
12
(½)
12
(½)
SILL 6(¼) THICK
66(2½)
1 SET OF LININGS
REQUIRED THUS
46(1¾)
8
(⅜)
20
(⅝)
5
(¼)
25
(⅞)
8
(⅜)
66(2½)
8
30
8
(⅜)
(1)
(⅜)
WINDOW W/W2 MADE
FROM PIECE CUT FROM
WALL B

WINDOW TYPE W/W2

COTTAGE DOLLS' HOUSE

SHEET 3

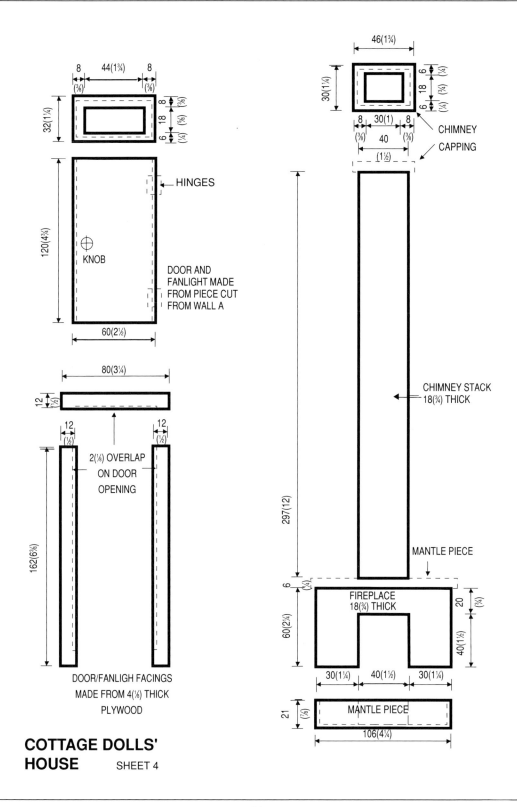

8
(⅜)
44(1¾)
8
(⅜)

32(1¼)

8
(⅜)
18
(⅝)
6
(¼)

HINGES

120(4¾)

⊕
KNOB

DOOR AND
FANLIGHT MADE
FROM PIECE CUT
FROM WALL A

60(2½)

80(3¼)

12
(½)

12
(½)

12
(½)

2(⅛) OVERLAP
ON DOOR
OPENING

162(6⅜)

DOOR/FANLIGH FACINGS
MADE FROM 4(⅛) THICK
PLYWOOD

46(1¾)

30(1¼)

6 (¼)
18 (¾)
6 (¼)

8
(⅜)
30(1)
8
(⅜)

40
(1½)

CHIMNEY

CAPPING

297(12)

CHIMNEY STACK
18(¾) THICK

MANTLE PIECE

6 (¼)

60(2¼)

FIREPLACE
18(¾) THICK

20 (¾)

40(1½)

30(1¼)
40(1½)
30(1¼)

21 (⅞)

MANTLE PIECE

106(4¼)

COTTAGE DOLLS'
HOUSE   SHEET 4

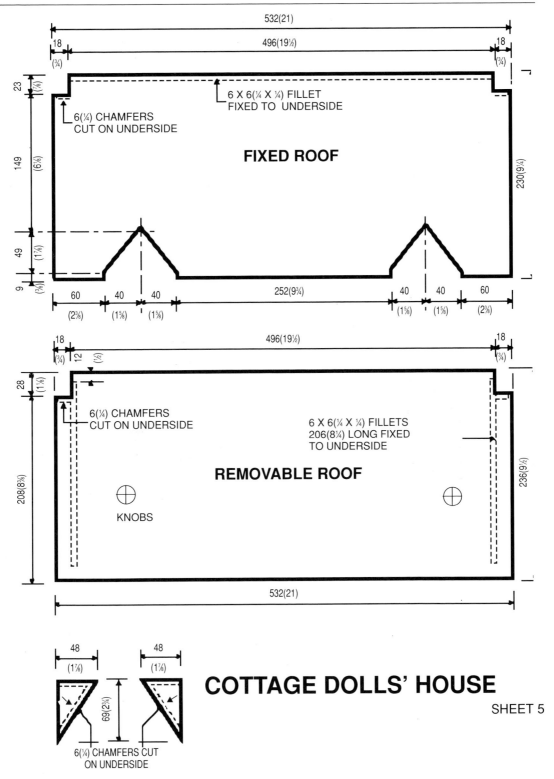

FIXED ROOF

532(21)

496(19½)

18 (¾)

23 (⅞)

6 X 6(¼ X ¼) FILLET
FIXED TO UNDERSIDE

6(¼) CHAMFERS
CUT ON UNDERSIDE

149 (6⅞)

230(9¼)

49 (1⅞)

9 (⅜)

60 (2⅜)   40 (1⅝)   40 (1⅝)   252(9¾)   40 (1⅝)   40 (1⅝)   60 (2⅜)

REMOVABLE ROOF

18 (¾)   12 (½)   496(19½)   18 (¾)

28 (1⅛)

6(¼) CHAMFERS
CUT ON UNDERSIDE

6 X 6(¼ X ¼) FILLETS
206(8¼) LONG FIXED
TO UNDERSIDE

208(8⅜)

236(9½)

⊕   ⊕
KNOBS

532(21)

48 (1⅞)   48 (1⅞)

69 (2¾)

6(¼) CHAMFERS CUT
ON UNDERSIDE

COTTAGE DOLLS' HOUSE

SHEET 5

GARAGE &
FILLING STATION

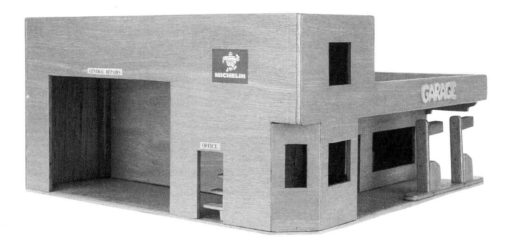

The manufacture of this toy provides an opportunity to gain further experience of cutting chamfers and also of constructing a simple but effective stair.

It is designed to suit the scale of the model cars and other forms of motor transport which provide so much pleasure for most children. In addition to the Forecourt with its filling pumps the accommodation includes a Showroom (with a novel 'up-and-over' door), a Workshop and a small Shop with a stair giving access to an office. The roof of the Showroom also provides car parking with access by way of a ramp.

CUTTING LIST

390 × 390 × 4 mm (15½ × 15½ × ⅛ in)   plywood or hardboard
1000 × 800 × 6 mm (40 × 32 × ¼ in)   plywood
170 × 36 × 4 mm (6¾ × 1½ × ⅛ in)   plywood
100 × 90 × 12 mm (4 × 3½ × ½ in)   timber
62 × 18 × 16 mm (2½ × ¾ × ⅝ in)   timber
5 mm (³⁄₁₆ in) diameter × 168 mm (6¾ in) dowel

CONSTRUCTION DETAILS

1. Mark and cut out the 4mm (⅛ in) thick base and mark on it the locations of the walls as illustrated in the plans.

2. Mark and cut out the components to form walls A, B, C, D, E, F, G, H, J and K. (Note that the design of this toy does not require that windows be made as described in Section 2, but simply to leave openings. However, if desired, windows can be made using the pieces cut out to form their openings, as previously described.)

3. Glue and pin a 6 × 6 mm (¼ × ¼ in) fillet 112 mm (4½ in) long to the Office side of wall B to provide a seating for the Office floor.

4. Cut out the Shop floor piece. Glue and fix this piece in its correct position against the base of wall B and pin through the wall into the edge of the floor piece to secure it.

5. Construct the small stair by cutting out the 12 mm (½ in) thick stepped stringer and the 7 No. 4 mm (⅛ in) thick treads. Glue and pin the treads to the stringer so that the right hand edges (facing up the stair) are flush with the edge of the stringer.

6. Fix the completed stair assembly to the Workshop side of wall B by glueing and pinning through the wall into the side of the stair stringer. Ensure that the stair is located so that the top edge of the stringer is flush with the bottom of the slot cut in wall B (below the Office door), and the bottom edge of the stringer is flush with the bottom edge of the wall.

7. Cut a 3 mm (⅛ in) chamfer on the edge of wall H where it will abut wall D. Glue and pin a length of 6 × 6 mm (¼ × ¼ in) fillet to the inside face of wall H to provide a seating for the Workshop roof. Note that a 12 mm (½ in) space is to be left at one end to accommodate a post, and the other end will terminate against wall B. Also glue and pin a length of 6 × 6 mm (¼ × ¼ in) fillet to the other side of this wall to provide a seating for the ramp. Mark on the wall the top surface of the ramp incline, as illustrated on the plans, and fix the fillet so that it is 6 mm (¼ in) below this line.

8. Glue and slot wall H into the slot cut in wall B for this purpose. Pin through wall H into the edge of wall B and into the edge of the Shop floor piece previously fixed to wall B.

9. Cut out the Office floor piece.

If the inside walls of the Shop are to be painted or varnished this is an opportune time to apply the desired finish to those parts of walls A, B, C, D, G and H which will enclose the Shop, as well as to the Shop floor and the underside of the Office floor piece, before further assembly takes place.

10. Glue the contact surfaces on the Office floor piece and slide the stair landing projection part of it through the slot under the door opening in wall B until the floor edge abuts the wall and is seated on the fillet fixed to wall B. Pin through walls B and H into the edges of the floor to secure it.

11. Cut 3 mm (⅛ in) chamfers along the edges of the Shop element of wall A where they will abut walls C and D.

Glue and pin lengths of 6 × 6 mm (¼ × ¼ in) fillet to the inside face of wall A to provide seatings for the Office floor and the Workshop roof. Note the requirement to leave a 6 mm ($\frac{1}{4}$ in) space at each end of the roof support fillet to accommodate the adjoining walls.

12. Glue and fix wall A into its position and pin through it into the edges of the Shop and Office floors, and wall H.

13. Cut a 3 mm ($\frac{1}{8}$ in) chamfer along the edge of the Shop element of wall G where it will abut wall C.

Glue and pin a length of 6 × 6 mm ($\frac{1}{4}$ × $\frac{1}{4}$ in) fillet to the inside face of wall G to provide a seating for the Workshop roof. Note that a 12 mm ($\frac{1}{2}$ in) space is to be left at one end to accommodate a post, and the other end will terminate against wall B.

14. Glue and pin wall G to the edges of wall B and the Shop and Office floors. Pin through wall A into the edge of wall G.

15. Fix two 12 × 12 mm ($\frac{1}{2}$ × $\frac{1}{2}$ in) posts to the inside face of wall E by glueing and pinning into them through the wall. Note that a 6 mm ($\frac{1}{4}$ in) space is left between the ends of the walls and the post sides to accommodate the adjoining walls. The post tops terminate at the underside of the Workshop roof.

Glue and pin a length of 6 × 6 mm ($\frac{1}{4}$ × $\frac{1}{4}$ in) fillet between the post tops to provide a seating for the Workshop roof.

16. Glue and pin wall E to the ends of walls G and H. Pin through walls G and H into the posts fixed to wall E.

17. Cut 3 mm ($\frac{1}{8}$ in) chamfers along the edges of walls C and D where they will abut walls A, G and H, and when satisfied that they neatly fit into their positions against these walls, glue them into place and pin through them into the edges of the Shop floor. They can be further

secured, if considered necessary, by pinning down through the Office floor into their top edges, but this operation will necessitate the use of a metal rod or similar extension placed on top of the pins by which to hammer them home.

18. Fix two 12 × 12 mm ($\frac{1}{2}$ × $\frac{1}{2}$ in) posts and a length of 6 × 6 mm ($\frac{1}{4}$ × $\frac{1}{4}$ in) fillet to the inside face of wall F all as described for the similar fixtures to wall E (*instruction 15*).

19. Glue and pin a length of 6 × 6 mm ($\frac{1}{4}$ × $\frac{1}{4}$ in) fillet to the inside face of wall J to provide a seating for the Showroom roof. Note the requirement to leave a 12 mm ($\frac{1}{2}$ in) space at one end to accommodate a post.

Glue and pin a length of 6 × 6 mm ($\frac{1}{4}$ × $\frac{1}{4}$ in) fillet to the other side to provide a seating for the ramp, all as described for the similar fixture to wall H (*instruction 7*).

20. Fix a 12 × 12 mm ($\frac{1}{2}$ × $\frac{1}{2}$ in) post to the inside face of wall K by glueing and pinning into it through the wall. Note the requirement to leave a 6 mm ($\frac{1}{4}$ in) space between the side of the post and the end of the wall where wall B will adjoin wall K. The top of the post terminates at the underside of the Showroom roof.

Glue and pin a length of 6 × 6 mm ($\frac{1}{4}$ × $\frac{1}{4}$ in) fillet to the inside face of wall K to provide a seating for the Showroom roof. The fillet abuts the post at one end and leaves a space of 12 mm ($\frac{1}{2}$ in) at its other end to accommodate the post fixed to wall F.

21. Cut out the 'up-and-over' door from the piece previously cut out of wall K to form the door opening. Assemble this door as follows:

i. Cut out the parts forming the door assembly, i.e. the door lintol, stops and brackets, as illustrated on the plans.

ii. Glue and pin the door lintel to the outside

face of wall K so that it is centred on the door opening and overhangs the opening top by 6 mm ($\frac{1}{4}$ in).

iii. Glue and pin the door stops to the inside face of wall K, one at each side of the bottom of the opening, so that each stop overhangs the opening side 3 mm ($\frac{1}{8}$ in).

iv. Glue and pin the smaller brackets to the inside face of the door, one at the top of each end.

v. Cut the length of 5 mm ($\frac{3}{16}$ in) diameter dowel and glue and thread it through the holes in the small brackets fixed to the door so that it projects 12 mm ($\frac{1}{2}$ in) each end.

vi. Fix a small door knob (made as described in Project 10 – the Corner Shop) to the outside face of the door.

vii. Glue and pin one of the larger brackets to the inside face of wall K at the top of one of the sides of the door opening.

viii. lace the door in its assembled position by inserting a projecting end of the dowel through the hole in the larger bracket fixed to the top side of the door opening. Thread the other larger bracket onto the other projection end of the dowel, and holding the bracket in its position at the other top side of the door opening, ensure that the door rotates freely into the open and closed position. When satisfied, glue and pin the larger bracket into its position at the top side of the door opening. Note that it might be necessary to slightly enlarge the holes cut in the larger brackets to allow the dowel to rotate freely, but with sufficient friction to ensure that the door will be retained in its open position.

22. Glue and pin wall F to the edge of wall J. Pin through wall J into the post previously fixed to wall F.

23. Glue and pin wall F to the edge of wall K. Pin through wall K into the post previously fixed to wall F.

24. Secure the assembly of walls F, J and K to the assembly previously completed by glueing the contact surfaces and pinning through wall K into the edge of wall B; through wall B into the post previously fixed to wall K; through wall B into the edge of wall J; and through the parapet end of wall A into the parapet projection edge of wall K. (Note that a length of fillet, if previously fixed to the inside face of wall B along a line of the adjoining edge of wall J, will help to determine the location of wall J against wall B when executing this instruction).

25. Locate the assembly so far completed onto the base and confirm the location of the holes required for the screw fixings into the bottoms of the 12 × 12 mm ($\frac{1}{2}$ × $\frac{1}{2}$ in) posts.

This is an opportune time to paint or varnish the interior of the Office before fixing the Workshop roof.

26. Mark and cut out the components for the Workshop and Showroom roofs, and the ramp.

27. Glue around the walls in the locations which will be in contact with the Workshop roof and lower it into its position seated on the fillets previously fixed to the walls for this purpose. Secure it by pinning into its edges through walls A, E, G and H.

28. Glue and position the Showroom roof as for the Workshop roof and secure it by pinning into its edges through walls A, F, J and K.

29. Cut the chamfers at each end of the underside of the ramp.

Glue along the locations on walls H and J which will be in contact with the ramp and lower it into its position seated on the fillets previously fixed to the walls for this purpose. Secure the ramp by pinning into its edges through walls H and J.

This is an opportune time to paint or varnish the interior of the Workshop and Showroom before fixing the assembly to the base.

30. Cut out the pieces to make the two pump units and the island base. Assemble each pump unit by glueing and pinning the 12 mm ($\frac{1}{2}$ in) and 16 mm ($\frac{5}{8}$ in) thick pieces to the vertical post as illustrated in the plans. Fix the completed pump units to the island base by glueing and screwing through it into the bottoms of the pump units using a $\frac{5}{8}$ in × 4 countersunk (c/s) screw for each.

At this stage paint or varnish the pump unit assembly and the main base.

31. Fix the pump unit assembly to the base in its correct position by glueing and screwing

through the base into the bottom of the assembly using 2 No. $\frac{1}{2}$ in × 4 c/s screws (ensure that these screws are located so that they will drive through the island base into the bottoms of the two pump units – missing the screws which were used to fix the units to the island base!).

32. Secure the garage assembly to the base by glueing and screwing through the base into the bottoms of the 12 × 12 mm ($\frac{1}{2}$ × $\frac{1}{2}$ in) posts using 5 No. $\frac{5}{8}$ in × 4 c/s screws, and into the bottom of the shop floor using a $\frac{1}{4}$ in × 4 c/s screw.

33. Cut out the 'GARAGE' motif from 4 mm ($\frac{1}{8}$ in) thick plywood and glue and pin it to the parapet face of wall A centred over the Forecourt.

34. Complete the toy by applying the desired finish of paint, varnish or patterned paper, or combinations of these, to the external surfaces.

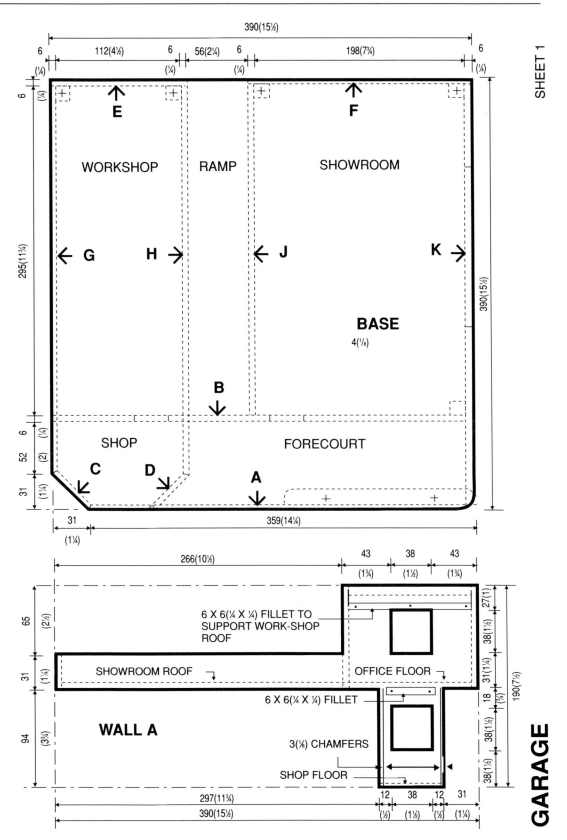

390(15½)

6

112(4½)

6

56(2¼)

6

198(7¾)

6

(¼)

(¼)

(¼)

(¼)

6

(¼)

E

F

WORKSHOP

RAMP

SHOWROOM

295(11¾)

390(15½)

G

H →

← J

K →

BASE

4(⅛)

B

SHOP

FORECOURT

6

(¼)

52

(2)

C

D

A

31

(1¼)

31

359(14¼)

(1¼)

266(10½)

43

(1¾)

38

(1½)

43

(1¾)

65

(2½)

27(1)

6 X 6(¼ X ¼) FILLET TO
SUPPORT WORK-SHOP
ROOF

38(1½)

31

(1¼)

SHOWROOM ROOF

OFFICE FLOOR

31(1¼)

190(7½)

18

(¾)

6 X 6(¼ X ¼) FILLET

94

(3¾)

WALL A

38(1½)

3(⅛) CHAMFERS

38(1½)

SHOP FLOOR

297(11¾)

12

38

12

31

390(15½)

(½)

(1½)

(½)

(1¼)

GARAGE

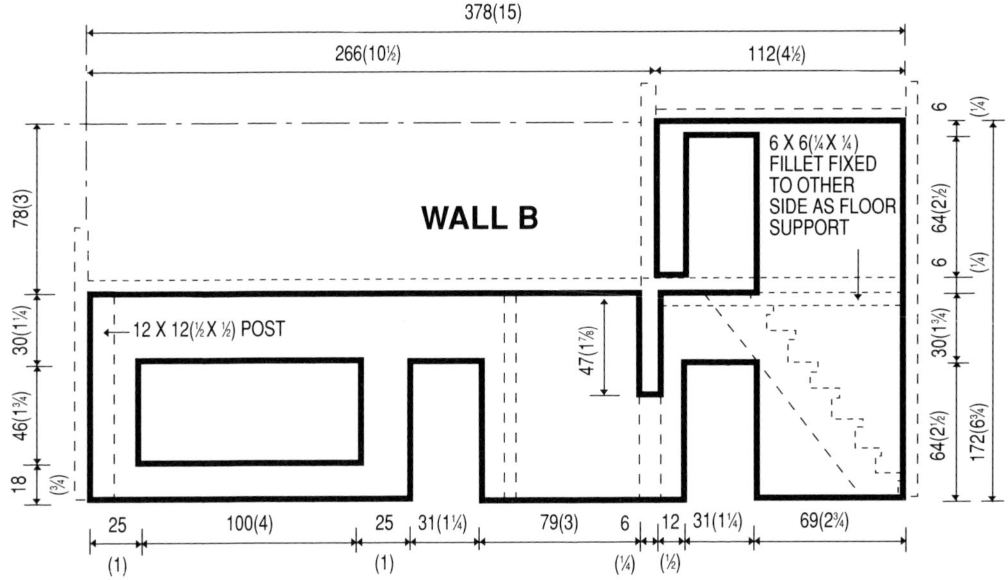
378(15)
266(10½)
112(4½)
WALL B
6 X 6(¼ X ¼) FILLET FIXED TO OTHER SIDE AS FLOOR SUPPORT
12 X 12(½ X ½) POST
47(1⅞)
78(3)
30(1¼)
46(1¾)
18
(¾)
6
(¼)
64(2½)
6
(¼)
30(1¼)
64(2½)
172(6¾)
25
(1)
100(4)
25
(1)
31(1¼)
79(3)
6
(¼)
12
(½)
31(1¼)
69(2¾)

SHEET 2

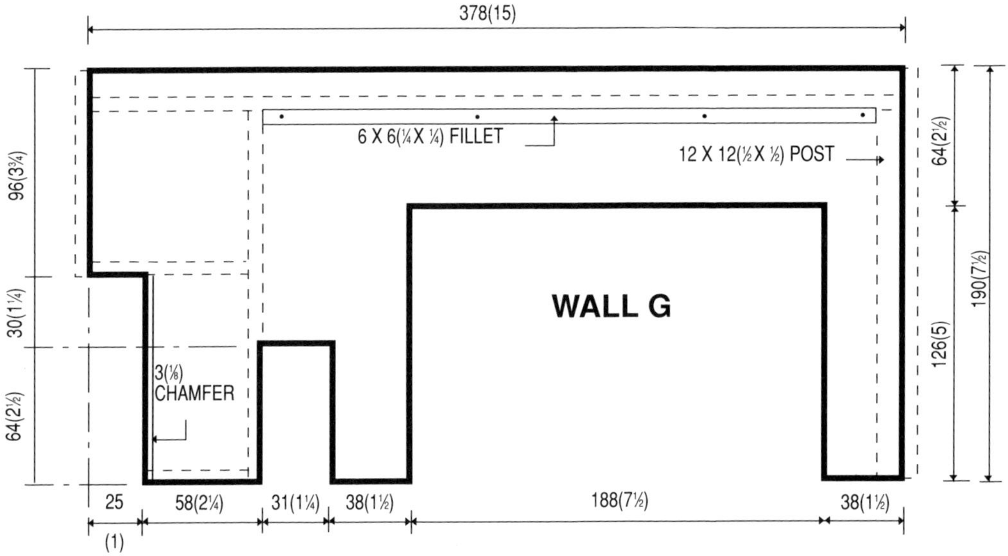
378(15)
6 X 6(¼ X ¼) FILLET
12 X 12(½ X ½) POST
WALL G
3(⅛) CHAMFER
96(3¾)
30(1¼)
64(2½)
64(2½)
126(5)
190(7½)
25
(1)
58(2¼)
31(1¼)
38(1½)
188(7½)
38(1½)

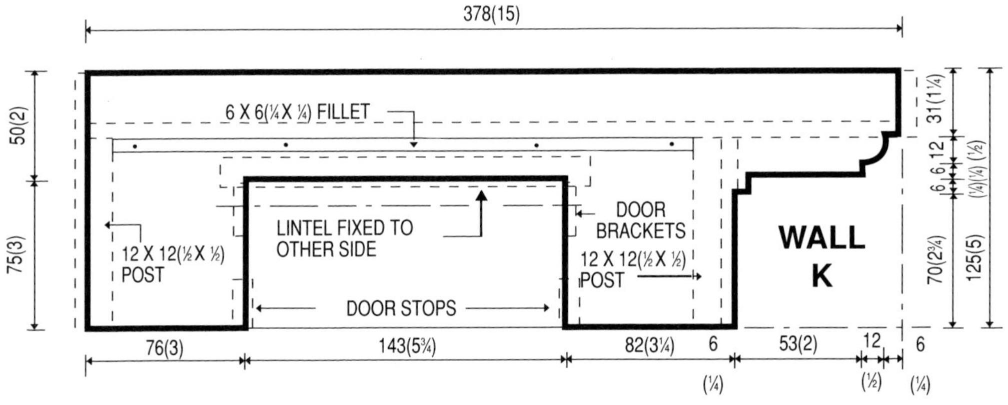
378(15)
6 X 6(¼ X ¼) FILLET
LINTEL FIXED TO OTHER SIDE
DOOR BRACKETS
12 X 12(½ X ½) POST
12 X 12(½ X ½) POST
DOOR STOPS
WALL K
50(2)
75(3)
31(1¼)
12
(½)
6
(¼)
6
(¼)
70(2¾)
125(5)
76(3)
143(5¾)
82(3¼)
6
(¼)
53(2)
12
(½)
6
(¼)

GARAGE

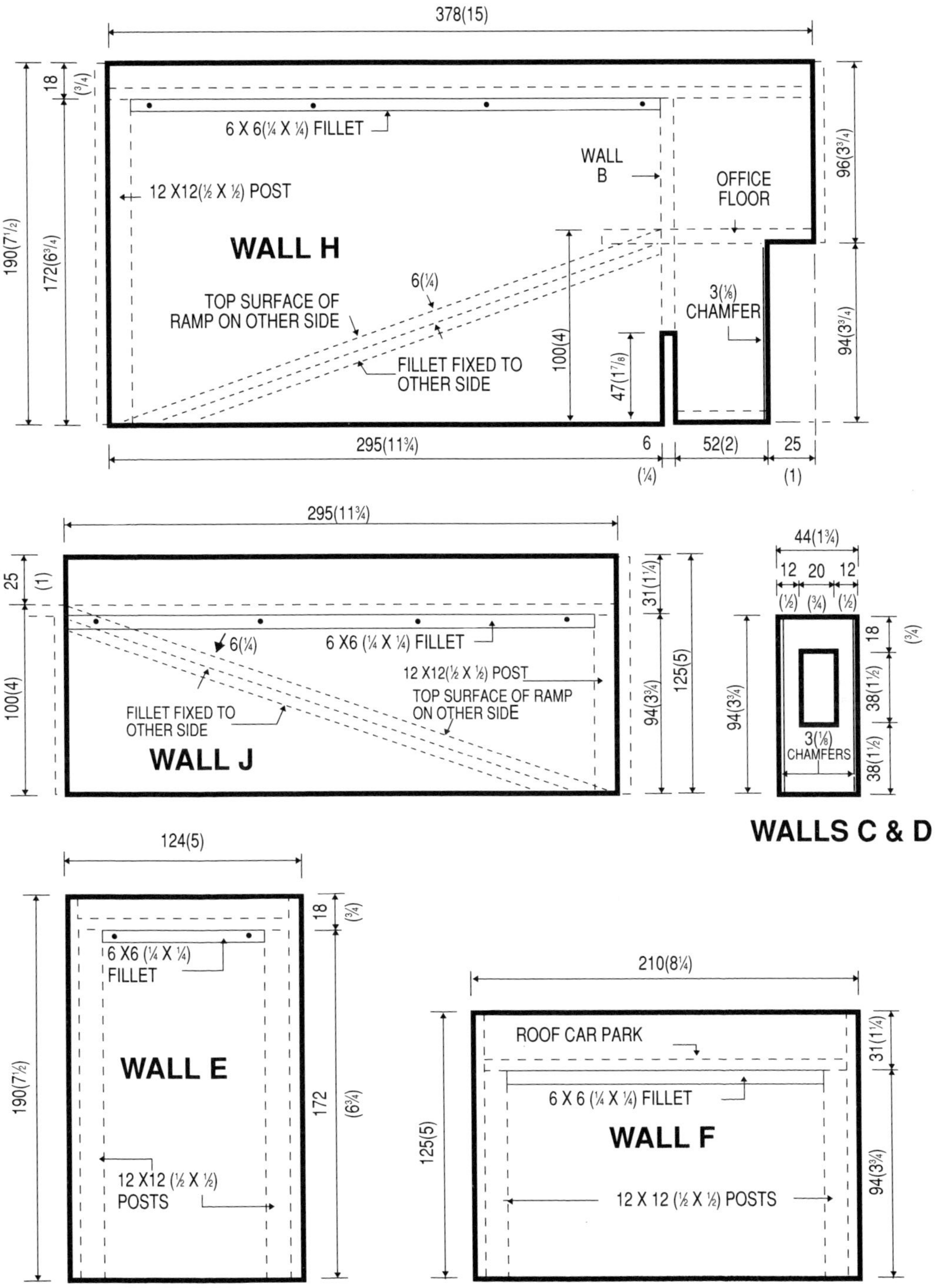
378(15)
6 X 6(¼ X ¼) FILLET
WALL B
12 X12(½ X ½) POST
OFFICE FLOOR
WALL H
6(¼)
TOP SURFACE OF RAMP ON OTHER SIDE
3(⅛) CHAMFER
FILLET FIXED TO OTHER SIDE
100(4)
47(1⅞)
190(7½)
172(6¾)
18
(¾)
96(3¾)
94(3¾)
295(11¾)
6
(¼)
52(2)
25
(1)
295(11¾)
25
(1)
100(4)
6(¼)
6 X6 (¼ X ¼) FILLET
12 X12(½ X ½) POST
TOP SURFACE OF RAMP ON OTHER SIDE
FILLET FIXED TO OTHER SIDE
WALL J
31(1¼)
94(3¾)
125(5)
44(1¾)
12 20 12
(½) (¾) (½)
94(3¾)
18
(¾)
38(1½)
38(1½)
3(⅛) CHAMFERS
WALLS C & D
124(5)
6 X6 (¼ X ¼) FILLET
WALL E
12 X12 (½ X ½) POSTS
190(7½)
18
(¾)
172
(6¾)
210(8¼)
ROOF CAR PARK
6 X 6 (¼ X ¼) FILLET
WALL F
12 X 12 (½ X ½) POSTS
125(5)
31(1¼)
94(3¾)

GARAGE

SHEET 3

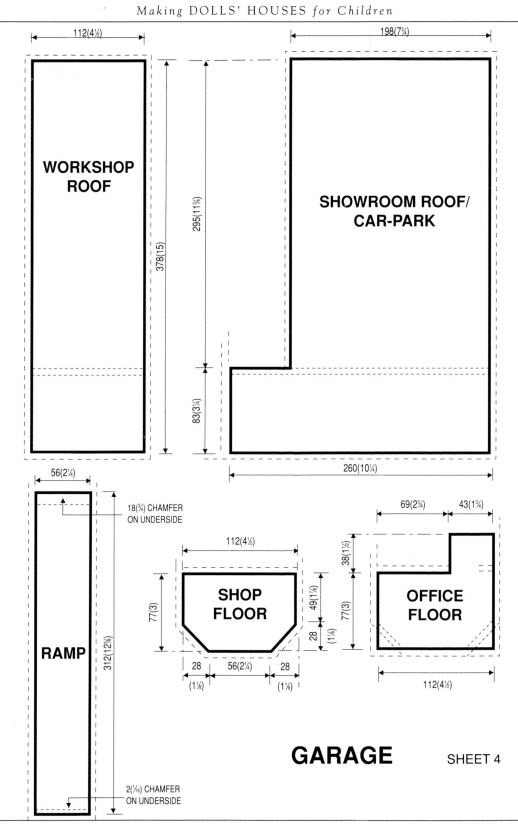

112(4½)

198(7¾)

WORKSHOP ROOF

SHOWROOM ROOF/ CAR-PARK

378(15)

295(11¾)

83(3¼)

260(10¼)

56(2¼)

18(¾) CHAMFER ON UNDERSIDE

69(2¾)

43(1¾)

112(4½)

38(1½)

77(3)

SHOP FLOOR

49(1⅞)

OFFICE FLOOR

77(3)

28
(1⅛)

RAMP

312(12⅜)

28
(1⅛)

56(2¼)

28
(1⅛)

112(4½)

GARAGE   SHEET 4

2(¹⁄₁₆) CHAMFER ON UNDERSIDE

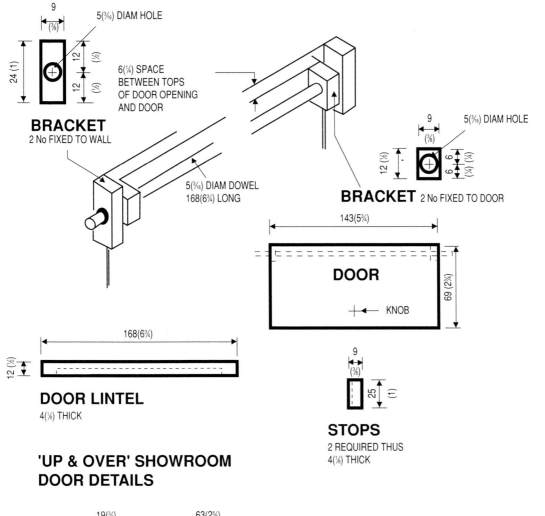

9
(⅜)

5(³⁄₁₆) DIAM HOLE

24 (1)

12 (½)

12 (½)

BRACKET
2 No FIXED TO WALL

6(¼) SPACE
BETWEEN TOPS
OF DOOR OPENING
AND DOOR

5(³⁄₁₆) DIAM DOWEL
168(6¾) LONG

9
(⅜)

5(³⁄₁₆) DIAM HOLE

12 (½)

6 (¼)

6 (¼)

BRACKET 2 No FIXED TO DOOR

143(5¾)

DOOR

69 (2¾)

KNOB

168(6¾)

12 (½)

DOOR LINTEL

4(⅛) THICK

9
(⅜)

25 (1)

STOPS

2 REQUIRED THUS
4(⅛) THICK

'UP & OVER' SHOWROOM DOOR DETAILS

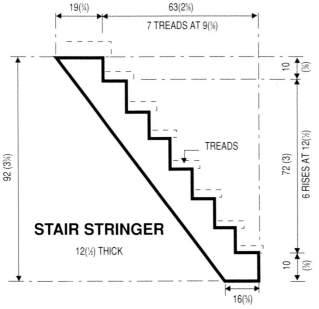

19(¾)

63(2⅝)

7 TREADS AT 9(⅜)

10 (⅜)

72 (3)

6 RISES AT 12(½)

10 (⅜)

92 (3¾)

TREADS

STAIR STRINGER

12(½) THICK

16(⅝)

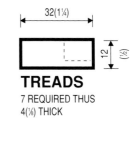

32(1¼)

12 (½)

TREADS

7 REQUIRED THUS
4(⅛) THICK

STAIR DETAILS

GARAGE SHEET 5

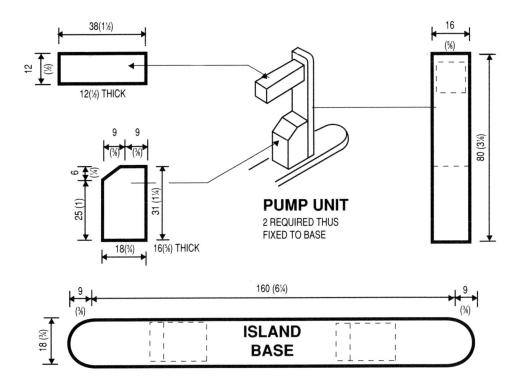

38(1½)
12
(½)
12(½) THICK
16
(⅝)
80 (3⅛)
9 9
(⅜) (⅜)
6
(¼)
25 (1)
31 (1¼)
18(¾)
16(⅝) THICK
PUMP UNIT
2 REQUIRED THUS
FIXED TO BASE
9
(⅜)
160 (6¼)
9
(⅜)
18 (¾)
ISLAND
BASE
80(3⅛)
GARAGE
18 (¾)
MOTIF
4 (⅛) THICK

GARAGE

SHEET 6

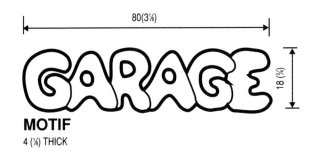

PROJECT 4

'WOODLAND COTTAGE' DOLLS' HOUSE

This Dolls' House was designed to accommodate a family of woodland creatures (bears, rabbits and mice) which are obtainable in toy shops in the United Kingdom and which are very popular with younger children. Accordingly, the house is scaled to suit the size of the creatures – door openings will accommodate the size of the largest animal – a bear.

The kitchen is provided with a novelty in the form of 'built-in' cupboard units including a high-level unit.

Access is by way of removable roofs which can be put aside whilst the toy is being played with. This is considered a more suitable form of access for the younger child than if the roofs were to be hinged.

A feature of this toy is its structural strength which is achieved by the formation of 'box beam' to which a handle is attached affording easy lifting and carrying. The handle is so shaped that it does not detract from the pleasing appearance of the toy.

CUTTING LIST

475 × 450 × 12 mm (19 × 18 × $\frac{1}{2}$ ins)	plywood
1200 × 1200 × 6 mm (48 × 48 × $\frac{1}{4}$ in)	plywood
400 × 150 × 12 mm (16 × 6 × $\frac{1}{2}$ in)	timber
515 × 60 × 19 mm (20$\frac{1}{2}$ × 2$\frac{1}{2}$ × $\frac{3}{4}$ in)	timber
325 × 45 × 25 mm (13 × 1$\frac{3}{4}$ × 1 in)	timber
6 × 6 × 975 mm ($\frac{1}{4}$ × $\frac{1}{4}$ × 38$\frac{1}{2}$ in)	timber fillet

ANCILLARIES

2 pairs small knobs

CONSTRUCTION DETAILS

1. Mark and cut out the base; walls A, B, C, D, E, F, G, H, J, K and M; and piece L.

2. Using the pieces cut out to form the window openings in walls A, B, D, E, F and G, make the six windows (4 No. type W1 and 2 No. type W2). Paint or stain these and lay them aside to dry. (*See detailed instructions in Section 2*).

3. Cut out the parts required to make the 'box beam', ie piece N and the two 400 × 75 × 12 mm (16 × 3 × $\frac{1}{2}$ in) pieces.

4. Construct the 'box beam' by glueing and pinning piece N to the two 12 mm ($\frac{1}{2}$ in) thick pieces. Then glue and pin wall J to the other edges of the two 12 mm ($\frac{1}{2}$ in) thick pieces, all as indicated on the Detail Section in the plans. Ensure that the beam is true and square before putting it aside for the glue to set.

5. Glue the windows into the openings in the walls from which they were originally cut.

6. Glue and screw wall B to the base, using 2 No. $\frac{5}{8}$ in × 4 countersunk (c/s) screws.

7. Glue and pin wall A to the end of the assembly of wall J and the 'box beam'.

8. Glue and screw wall A (with the assembly of wall J and 'box beam') to the base. Pin through wall B into the end of wall J. Use 3 No. $\frac{5}{8}$ in × 4 c/s screws.

9. Glue and screw wall D to the base and pin through it into the ends of walls A and B. Use 3 No. $\frac{5}{8}$ in × 4 c/s screws.

10. Fix the two walls K by glueing and pinning into them through walls D and J.

11. Fix the 6 × 6 mm ($\frac{1}{4}$ × $\frac{1}{4}$) fillet to wall F (to support roof R) and glue and screw this wall to the base, using 2 No. $\frac{5}{8}$ in × 4 c/s screws.

12. Glue and screw wall C (with its chamfered top) to the base and pin through it into the end of wall B. Pin through wall F into the end of wall C. Use one $\frac{5}{8}$ in × 4 c/s screw.

13. Cut out the parts for the kitchen units, i.e. the worktop; pieces W and X (out of 25 mm (1 in) thick timber); fronts Y and Z; and the high level cupboard unit (out of 19 mm ($\frac{3}{4}$ in) thick timber). Construct the low level unit as follows:

i. glue and screw piece X to the end of piece W, using one 1$\frac{1}{2}$ in × 8 c/s screw.

ii. glue and pin front Y to the face of piece X with the top edges flush with each other.

iii. glue and pin front Z to the face of piece W with the top edges flush with each other.

iv. glue and pin the worktop onto the assembly so far made to complete it.

14. Glue and pin piece L to the top end of wall M so that when assembled it will span between walls M and J.

15. Glue and pin through wall H into the end of wall M (with piece L).

16. Glue and fix the high level cupboard unit into its position on wall H and pin into it through walls H and M.

17. Glue and fix the low level kitchen unit into its position on wall H and pin into it through walls H and M.

18. Glue and fix into position on the base the assembly of walls H and M with piece L and the kitchen units and secure it by pinning through wall J into the end of piece L, and through wall A into the end of the low level kitchen unit.

19. Glue and screw wall E to the base and pin through it into the ends of walls A, F and H. Use 4 No. $\frac{5}{8}$ in × 4 c/s screws.

20. Glue and fix into position wall G and pin into its ends through walls F and H.

21. Cut out plate S and the handle (19 mm ($\frac{3}{4}$ in) thick timber). Glue and secure the handle to the top of the plate by screwing into it through the plate from its underside, using 2 No. 1 in × 6 c/s screws.

22. Glue and screw the assembly of plate S with the handle onto the top of the 'box beam' (*see Detail Section on the plans*). Use 8 No. $\frac{1}{2}$ in × 4 c/s screws.

23. Mark and cut out the roofs P, Q and R.

24. Glue and pin roof R into its location over walls B and C with one of its edges supported on the fillet fixed to wall F.

25. Glue and pin the 6 × 6 ($\frac{1}{4}$ × $\frac{1}{4}$ in) fillets to the undersides of roofs P and Q ensuring that they are positioned in such a way as to properly locate the roofs when they are seated on the house. Fix two small knobs to the top surface of each of roofs P and Q to facilitate the lifting and placing of them.

26. Complete the fabrication of the house by glueing and pinning a plinth, made from 15 × 6 ($\frac{5}{8}$ × $\frac{1}{4}$ in) strips of plywood, around the base of the house. This will cover the heads of the fixing screws.

27. Complete the house by applying the desired finish of paint and/or varnish.

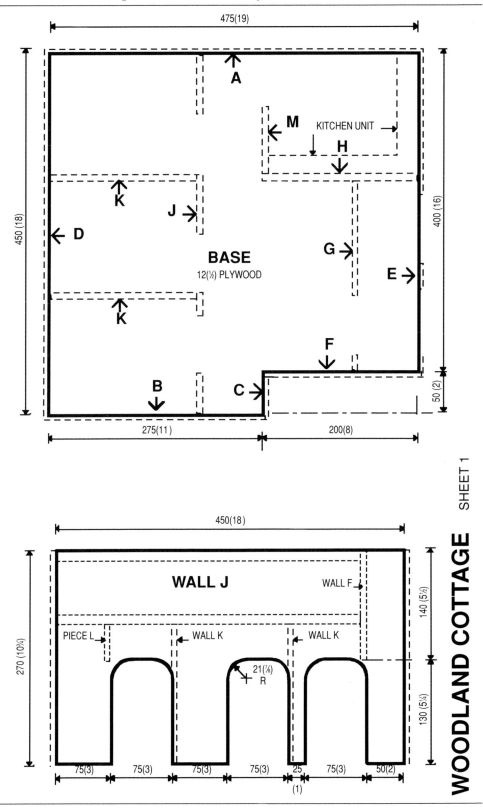

475(19)

450 (18)

A

M KITCHEN UNIT

H

400 (16)

K

J

D

G

BASE
12(½) PLYWOOD

E

K

F

E

B

C

50 (2)

275(11) 200(8)

450(18)

WALL J

WALL F

270 (10¾)

140 (5½)

PIECE L WALL K WALL K

21(⅞)
R

130 (5¼)

75(3) 75(3) 75(3) 75(3) 25 75(3) 50(2)

(1)

WOODLAND COTTAGE SHEET 1

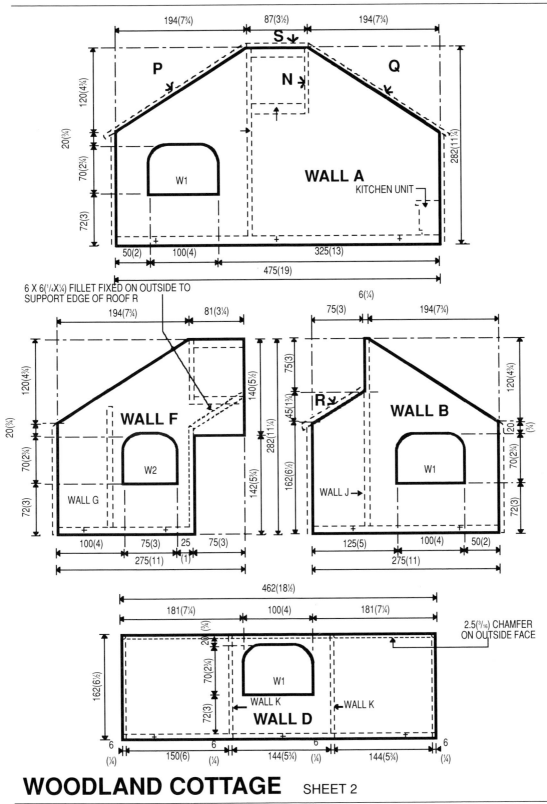

194(7¾) 87(3½) 194(7¾)

S↓

P↓ Q↓
N↓

120(4¾)
20(¾)
70(2¾)

W1

WALL A
KITCHEN UNIT↓

72(3)

50(2) 100(4) 325(13)

282(11¼)

475(19)

6 X 6(¼X¼) FILLET FIXED ON OUTSIDE TO
SUPPORT EDGE OF ROOF R

6(¼)

194(7¾) 81(3¼) 75(3) 194(7¾)

75(3)

120(4¾) 140(5½) 120(4¾)

20(¾)
R↓ 20(¾)
45(1¾)

WALL F
282(11¼)

70(2¾) W2 162(6½) **WALL B** 70(2¾)

282(11¼) W1

WALL G 142(5¾) WALL J→ 72(3)

72(3)

100(4) 75(3) 25 75(3) 125(5) 100(4) 50(2)

275(11) (1) 275(11)

462(18½)

181(7¼) 100(4) 181(7¼)

2.5(³/₁₆) CHAMFER
ON OUTSIDE FACE

20(¾)

162(6½) 70(2¾)

W1

72(3) WALL K← →WALL K

WALL D

6 6 6 6
(¼) 150(6) (¼) 144(5¾) (¼) 144(5¾) (¼)

WOODLAND COTTAGE SHEET 2

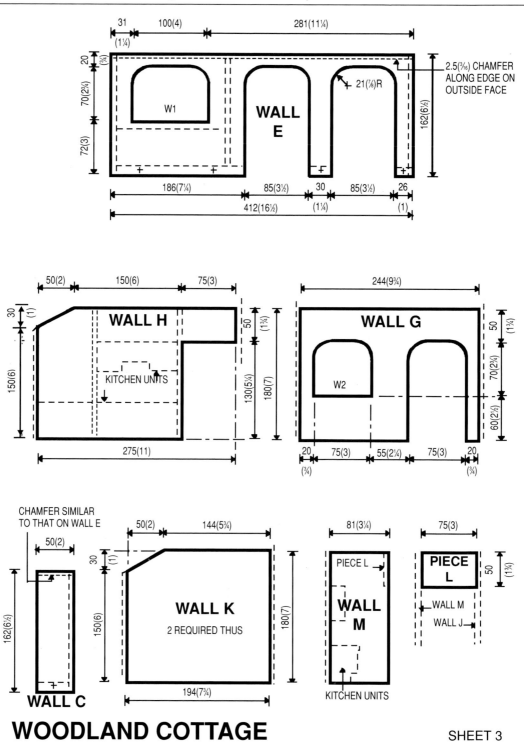

31 (1¼) 100(4) 281(11¼)

20 (¾)

70(2¾)

W1

WALL E

2.5(³⁄₁₆) CHAMFER ALONG EDGE ON OUTSIDE FACE

21(⁷⁄₈)R

162(6½)

72(3)

186(7¼) 85(3½) 30 85(3½) 26

412(16½) (1¼) (1)

50(2) 150(6) 75(3)

30 (1)

WALL H

50 (1¾)

KITCHEN UNITS

150(6)

130(5¼) 180(7)

275(11)

244(9¾)

WALL G

50 (1¾)

W2

70(2¾)

60(2½)

20 (¾) 75(3) 55(2¼) 75(3) 20 (¾)

CHAMFER SIMILAR TO THAT ON WALL E

50(2)

50(2) 144(5¾)

30 (1)

162(6½)

150(6)

WALL K

2 REQUIRED THUS

180(7)

194(7¾)

WALL C

81(3¼)

PIECE L

WALL M

KITCHEN UNITS

75(3)

PIECE L

50 (1¾)

WALL M

WALL J

WOODLAND COTTAGE

SHEET 3

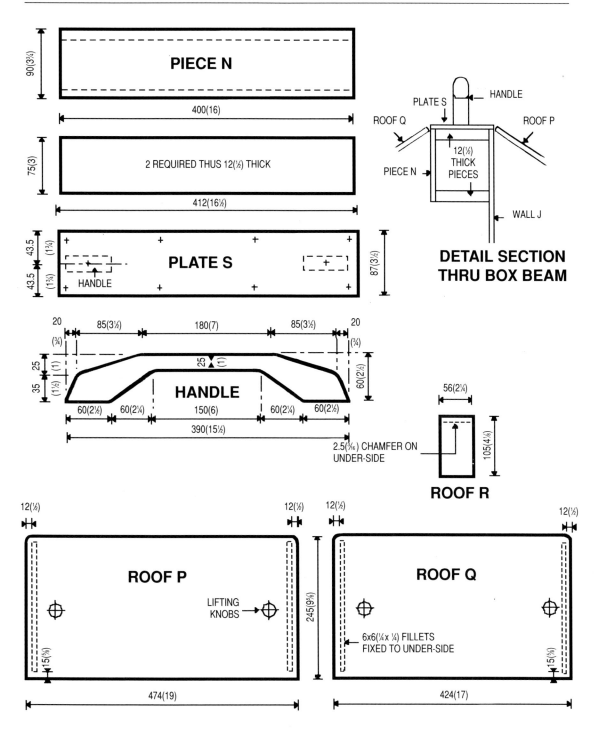

PIECE N

90(3¾)

400(16)

75(3)

2 REQUIRED THUS 12(½) THICK

412(16½)

43.5 (1¾)

43.5 (1¾)

PLATE S

87(3½)

HANDLE

PLATE S

HANDLE

ROOF Q

ROOF P

12(½) THICK PIECES

PIECE N

WALL J

DETAIL SECTION THRU BOX BEAM

20 (¾)

85(3½)

180(7)

85(3½)

20 (¾)

25 (1)

25

35 (1½)

60(2½)

HANDLE

60(2½)   60(2¼)

150(6)

60(2¼)   60(2½)

390(15½)

56(2¼)

105(4⅛)

2.5(³⁄₃₂) CHAMFER ON UNDER-SIDE

ROOF R

12(½)

12(½)

12(½)

12(½)

ROOF P

LIFTING KNOBS

245(9⅝)

15(⅝)

474(19)

ROOF Q

6x6(¼ x ¼) FILLETS FIXED TO UNDER-SIDE

15(⅝)

424(17)

WOODLAND COTTAGE

SHEET 4

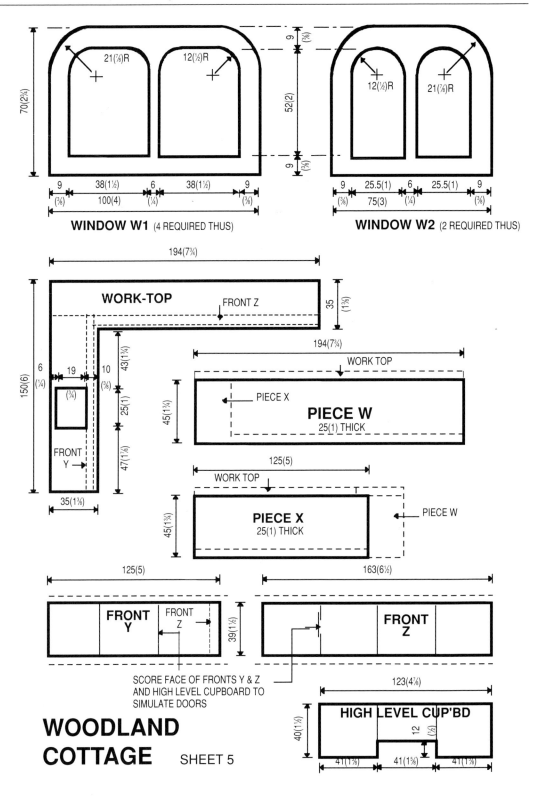

WINDOW W1 (4 REQUIRED THUS)

WINDOW W2 (2 REQUIRED THUS)

WORK-TOP

FRONT Z

PIECE W
25(1) THICK

PIECE X

PIECE X
25(1) THICK

PIECE W

FRONT Y

FRONT Z

FRONT Z

SCORE FACE OF FRONTS Y & Z
AND HIGH LEVEL CUPBOARD TO
SIMULATE DOORS

HIGH LEVEL CUP'BD

WOODLAND COTTAGE   SHEET 5

PROJECT 5

DOLLS' HOUSE – 'GABLES'

A s shown in the photograph of this toy, it was designed to suit a roof finished with cedar shingle tiles which were purchased in Vancouver, Canada. Obviously, the roofs need not be finished like this if there should be any difficulty in obtaining these tiles.

CUTTING LIST

2500 × 1200 × 6 mm (100 × 84 × $\frac{1}{4}$ in)	plywood
250 × 250 × 4 mm (10 × 10 × $\frac{1}{8}$ in)	plywood
75 × 50 × 25 mm (3 × 2 × 1 in)	timber
202 × 100 × 18 mm (8 × 4 × $\frac{3}{4}$ in)	timber
9 mm ($\frac{3}{8}$ in) diameter × 50 mm (2 in)	timber
6 × 6 × 2480 mm ($\frac{1}{4}$ × $\frac{1}{4}$ × 98 in)	timber fillet

ANCILLARIES

$1\frac{1}{2}$ pairs 25 mm (1 in) brass hinges

CONSTRUCTION DETAILS

1. Mark and cut out the components for the floors (Ground, First and Attic); walls A, B, C, D, E, and F; and piece G.

2. Complete the cutting of the windows, door and fanlight, using the pieces cut from the walls to form these. Stain or paint these elements and put them aside to dry. (*See also Window instructions in Section 2*).

3. Fix the 6 × 6 mm ($\frac{1}{4}$ × $\frac{1}{4}$ in) floor support fillets to walls A, B, C and D.

4. Cut out the parts forming the fireplace and fix them to wall D.

5. Cut out the parts forming the door lining and fix them to the outside face of wall B so that there is a 3 mm ($\frac{1}{8}$ in) overlap to the opening.

6. Glue the windows and fanlight into the openings in the walls from which they were originally cut.

7. Fix one pair of hinges to the door leaf and fix it into its opening in wall B so that it opens inwards with the stops formed by the overlap of the linings previously fixed (*see instruction 5*).

8. Glue and pin piece G to the underside of the Ground floor at its rear.

9. i. Cut out the components for the stair and construct it by glueing and pinning piece X to the stair base and pieces U and V to the base and to piece X.

ii. Glue the treads and risers to pieces U and V commencing with the bottom riser, then the bottom tread, the next riser, the next tread, *et seq* to completion.

iii. Glue and pin piece W to the side of stair piece V so that the profiles of the cut-outs to clear the door (when open) coincide on each piece.

iv. Glue and pin piece Y to piece W so that it overhangs the stair.

10. Glue and fix the completed stair assembly to wall E with its base flush with the bottom of wall E. Pin through E into piece Y.

11. At this point it is convenient to apply the desired finishes to the inside faces of all the walls and to the tops and undersides of the floors ensuring that the finish material is kept clear of the positions where walls/floors are fixed to each other. It is considerably more difficult to gain access to these surfaces when the house is fully assembled. Allow to dry.

12. Glue and pin the front wall B to the Ground floor, seated on the fillet previously fixed for this purpose.

13. Glue and pin the side wall A to the Ground floor and to the front wall B.

14. Glue and pin the side wall D to the Ground floor.

15. Glue and pin the front wall C to the Ground floor and to the side wall D.

16. Glue and slide wall E (with the stair assembly) into the first floor. (*See Section 2.*)

17. Glue and slide wall F into the First floor. (*See Joint instructions in Section 2.*)

18. Glue and insert the assembly of First floor with walls E and F and the stair, and pin to the Ground floor (from below) and to walls A, B, C and D. The First floor will be seated on the fillets previously fixed to the walls. Screw through the Ground floor into the base of the stair, using a $\frac{5}{8}$ in × 4 countersunk (c/s) screw.

19. Cut out the trap door from the Attic floor and refix it with a 25 mm (1 in) hinge.

20. Insert the Attic floor and glue and pin walls A, B, C and D to it. This floor will also be seated on the fillets previously fixed to the walls.

21. i. Mark and cut out the components forming the Verandah, i.e. the floor, front H, sides J and K, and piece L.

   ii. Glue and pin the 10 × 6 mm ($\frac{3}{8}$ × $\frac{1}{4}$ in) fillet to the underside of the floor at its rear.

   iii. Glue and slot the side J into the floor and pin the floor to it.

   iv. Glue and slot the front H into the floor and pin it to side J and pin the floor to it.

   v. Glue and pin piece L to side K and then glue and pin this assembly to the floor and to the front H.

   vi. Glue and pin the 20 × 6 mm ($\frac{3}{4}$ × $\frac{1}{4}$ in) chamfered fillet between the end pieces J and K.

   vii. Set aside this assembly to allow the glued joints to set firm.

22. Fix the assembled Verandah (minus roof) into its location against the front wall B by

glueing and screwing the fillets (items 21 ii and vi) to wall B and securing end wall K to wall E. Use 6 No $\frac{3}{8}$ in × 2 c/s screws to secure the fillets to wall B.

23. Mark and cut out the Verandah balustrades M and N and their cappings. This will be a convenient time to stain or paint the balustrades and lay aside to dry before fixing.

24. Mark and cut out the Verandah roof T and glue and pin it onto the Verandah assembly.

25. Glue the balustrades into their positions between the Verandah columns. Glue and slot the cappings between the columns and pin onto the balustrades.

26. Mark and cut out the roof parts P, Q, R and S and their respective barge-boards (including the barge-boards For the Verandah roof).

27. Cut out the parts forming the chimney assembly. Glue and screw the 25 mm (1 in) thick chimney stack in its correct location onto roof part Q, using a $\frac{3}{4}$ in × 4 c/s screw.

28. Fix roof part P by glueing and pinning it to the gables of walls A and D, first making any adjustments as necessary for the cut-out to fit the projection of the gable C.

29. Fix roof part Q (with chimney stack) by glueing and pinning it to the gables of walls A and D and to the top edge of roof part P.

30. Fix roof parts R and S after ensuring that the chamfers provide a good fit to each other at the ridge and to roof P. Glue and pin them to the gable of wall C and to roof P.

31. Glue and pin the chimney capping onto the stack and glue the dowel pots into the holes in the capping.

32. Glue and pin the barge-boards to the end edges of the roofs, including the Verandah roof. If roof tiles are to be fixed ensure that the barge-boards project above the roof surfaces by an amount equal to the thickness of the tiles.

33. If desired, fix the roof tiles starting at the bottom edges (eaves) and working in rows up to the top (ridge).

34. Complete the house by applying the desired finish.

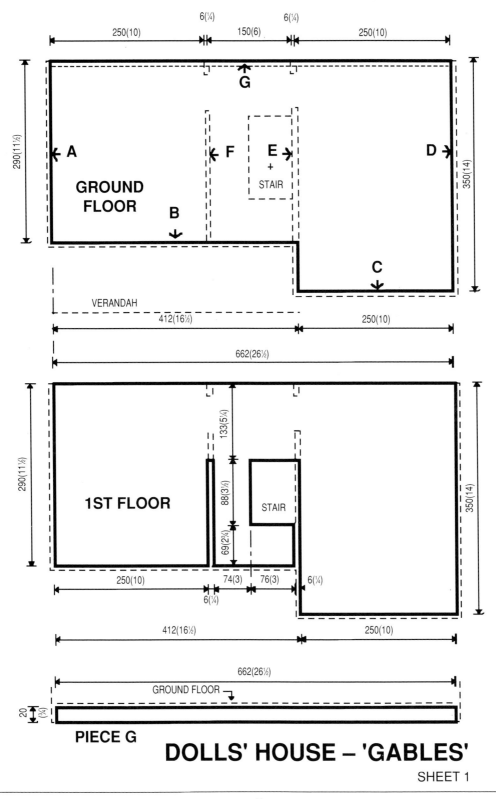

6(¼)　6(¼)
250(10)　150(6)　250(10)

290(11½)

A
GROUND FLOOR
F　**E**
+
STAIR
D
B
350(14)
G
C

VERANDAH
412(16½)　250(10)

662(26½)

290(11½)

1ST FLOOR
133(5¼)
88(3½)
69(2¾)
STAIR
350(14)

250(10)　74(3)　76(3)　6(¼)
6(¼)

412(16½)　250(10)

662(26½)

GROUND FLOOR

20 (¾)

PIECE G

DOLLS' HOUSE – 'GABLES'

SHEET 1

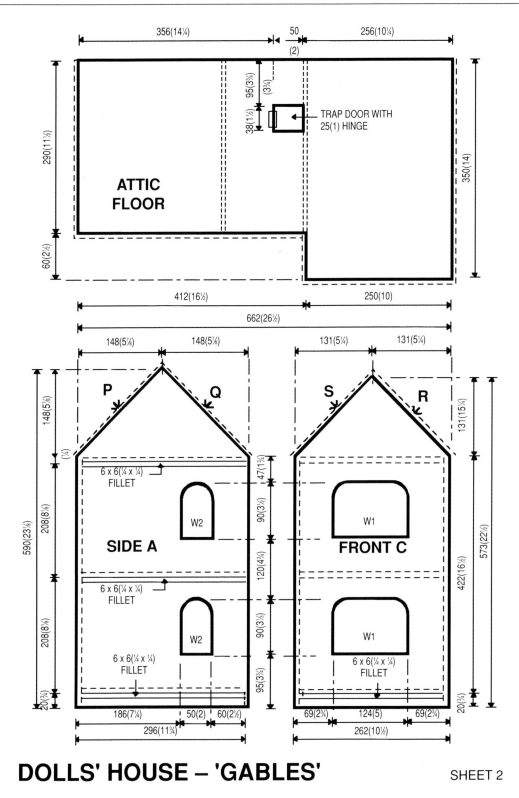

356(14¼)   50   256(10¼)
(2)

95(3¾)
(3¾)
38(1½)

TRAP DOOR WITH
25(1) HINGE

290(11½)   350(14)

**ATTIC
FLOOR**

60(2½)

412(16½)   250(10)

662(26½)

148(5⅞)   148(5⅞)   131(5¼)   131(5¼)

P   **Q**   **S**   **R**

148(5⅞)
(¼)
131(15¼)

47(1¾)

6 x 6(¼ x ¼)
FILLET

90(3½)

590(23⅛)   208(8⅛)

W2

SIDE A   **FRONT C**

W1

573(22½)

120(4¾)

6 x 6(¼ x ¼)
FILLET

422(16½)

208(8⅛)

90(3½)

W2

W1

6 x 6(¼ x ¼)
FILLET

95(3¾)

6 x 6(¼ x ¼)
FILLET

20(¾)

186(7¼)   50(2)   60(2½)   69(2¾)   124(5)   69(2¾)   20(¾)

296(11¾)   262(10½)

DOLLS' HOUSE – 'GABLES'

SHEET 2

70

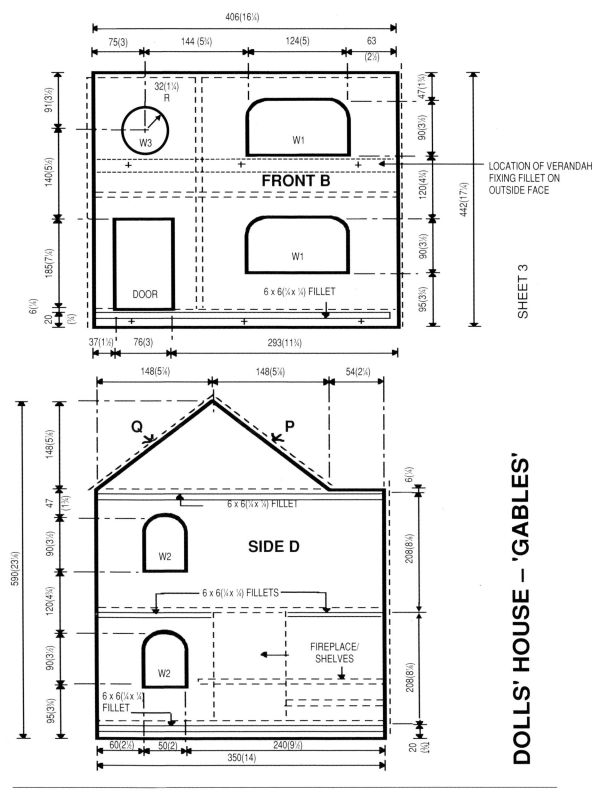

FRONT B

406(16¼)

75(3) 144 (5¾) 124(5) 63 (2½)

91(3½)

32(1¼) R

W3

140(5½)

47(1¾)

90(3½)

W1

LOCATION OF VERANDAH FIXING FILLET ON OUTSIDE FACE

120(4¾)

185(7¼)

90(3½)

W1

442(17¼)

DOOR

6 x 6(¼ x ¼) FILLET

95(3¾)

6(¼)

20 (¾)

37(1½) 76(3) 293(11¾)

SHEET 3

148(5⅞) 148(5⅞) 54(2¼)

Q P

148(5⅞)

6(¼)

47 (1¾)

6 x 6(¼ x ¼) FILLET

90(3½)

W2

SIDE D

208(8⅛)

590(23⅛)

120(4¾)

6 x 6(¼ x ¼) FILLETS

90(3½)

W2

FIREPLACE/ SHELVES

208(8⅛)

95(3¾)

6 x 6(¼ x ¼) FILLET

20 (¾)

60(2½) 50(2) 240(9½)

350(14)

DOLLS' HOUSE – 'GABLES'

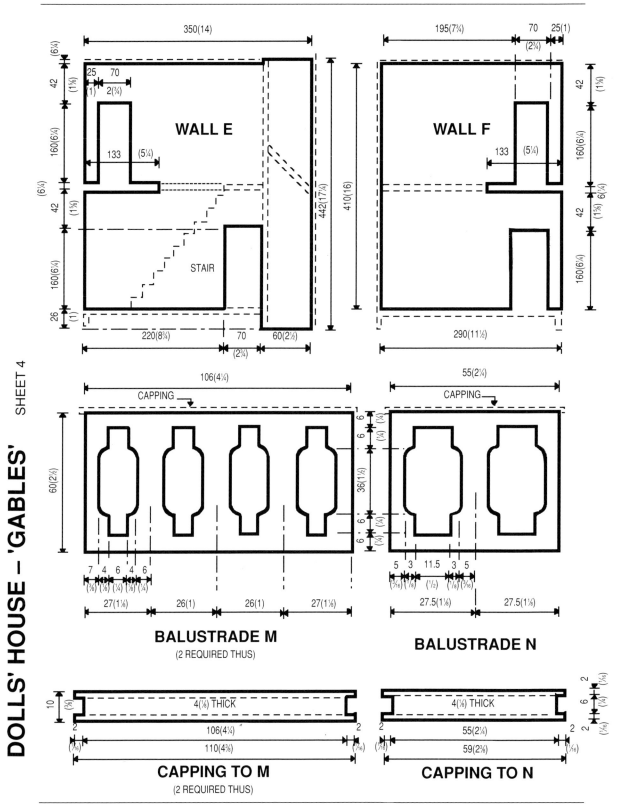

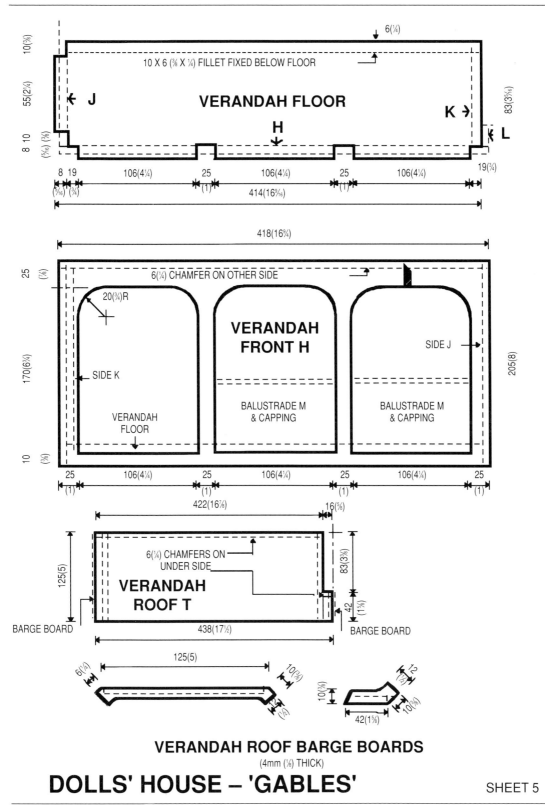

VERANDAH ROOF BARGE BOARDS
(4mm (⅛) THICK)

DOLLS' HOUSE – 'GABLES'

SHEET 5

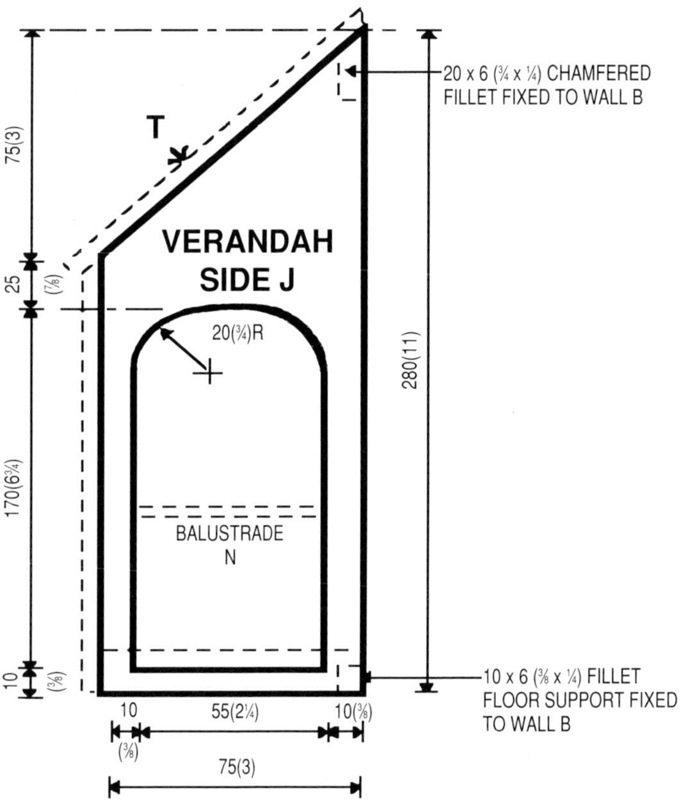
T
VERANDAH
SIDE J
75(3)
25
(⅞)
170(6¾)
10
(⅜)
20(¾)R
BALUSTRADE
N
280(11)
20 x 6 (¾ x ¼) CHAMFERED
FILLET FIXED TO WALL B
10 x 6 (⅜ x ¼) FILLET
FLOOR SUPPORT FIXED
TO WALL B
10
(⅜)
55(2¼)
10(⅜)
75(3)

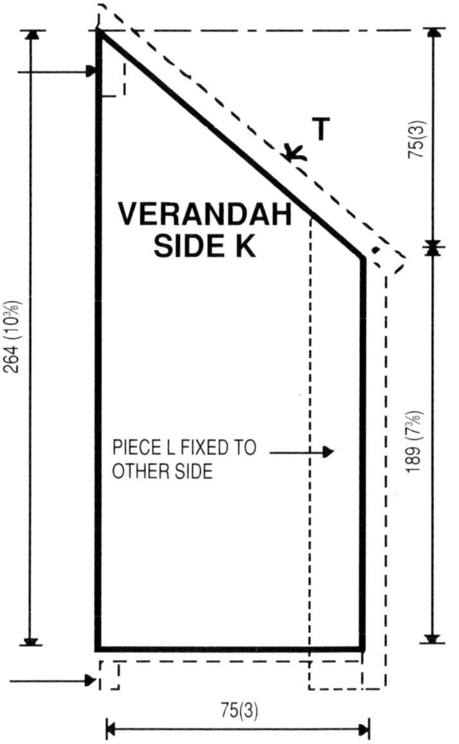
T
VERANDAH
SIDE K
264 (10⅜)
75(3)
189 (7⅜)
PIECE L FIXED TO
OTHER SIDE
75(3)

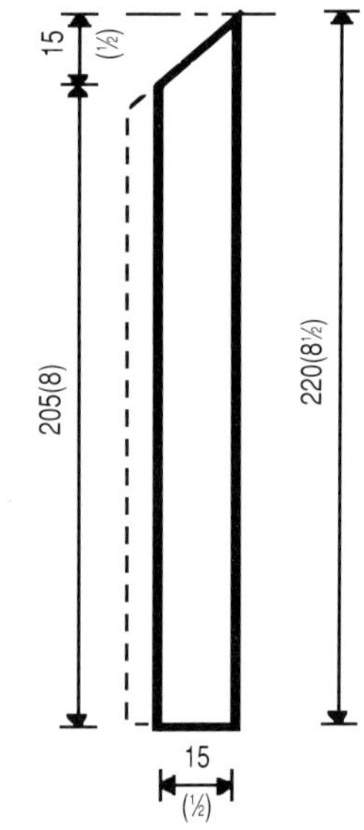
15
(½)
205(8)
220(8½)
15
(½)

PIECE L

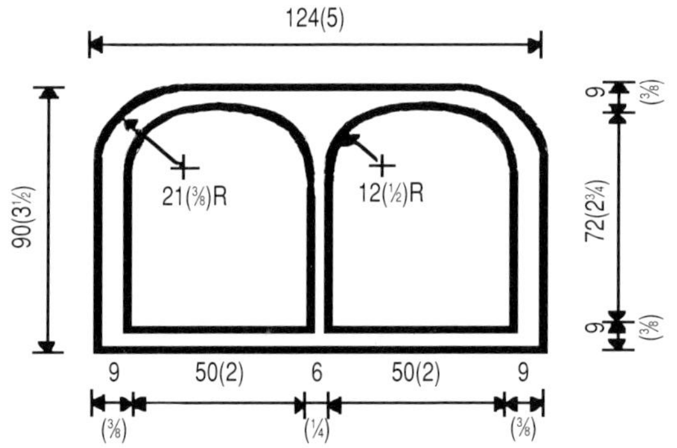
124(5)
90(3½)
21(⅜)R
12(½)R
9
(⅜)
72(2¾)
9
(⅜)
9
50(2)
6
50(2)
9
(⅜)
(¼)
(⅜)

WINDOW W1
4 REQUIRED THUS

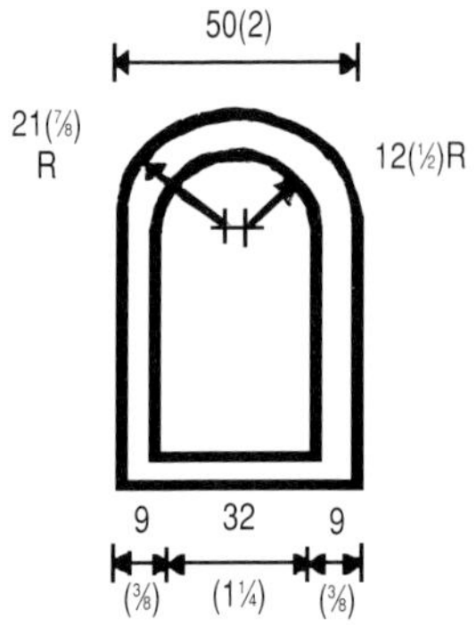
50(2)
21(⅞)
R
12(½)R
9
32
9
(⅜)
(1¼)
(⅜)

WINDOW W2
4 REQUIRED THUS

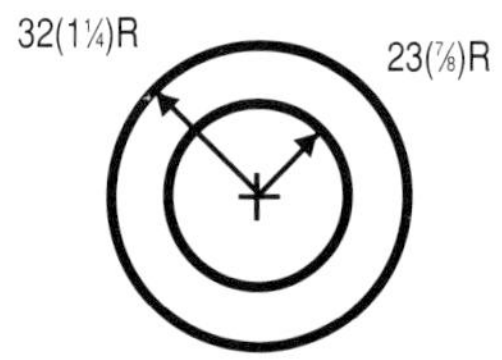
32(1¼)R
23(⅞)R

WINDOW W3

DOLLS' HOUSE – 'GABLES'

SHEET 6

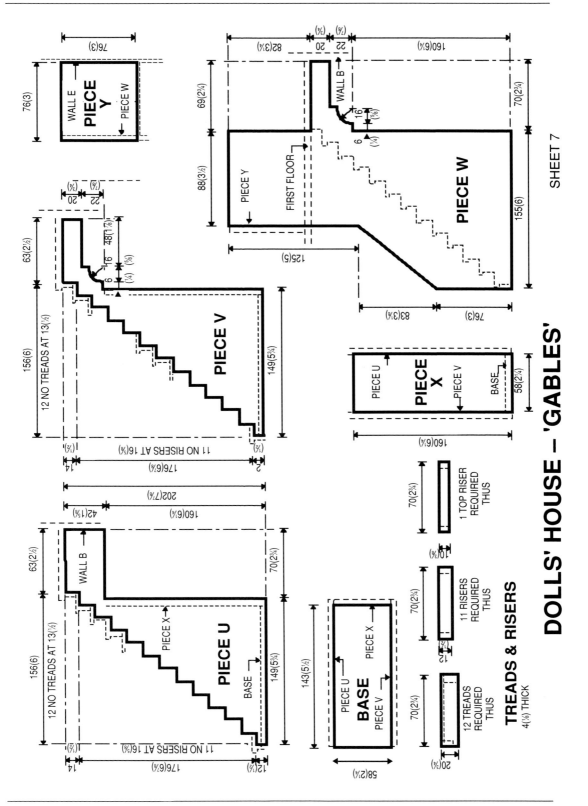

SHEET 7

DOLLS' HOUSE – 'GABLES'

TREADS & RISERS

4(⅛) THICK

1 TOP RISER REQUIRED THUS

11 RISERS REQUIRED THUS

12 TREADS REQUIRED THUS

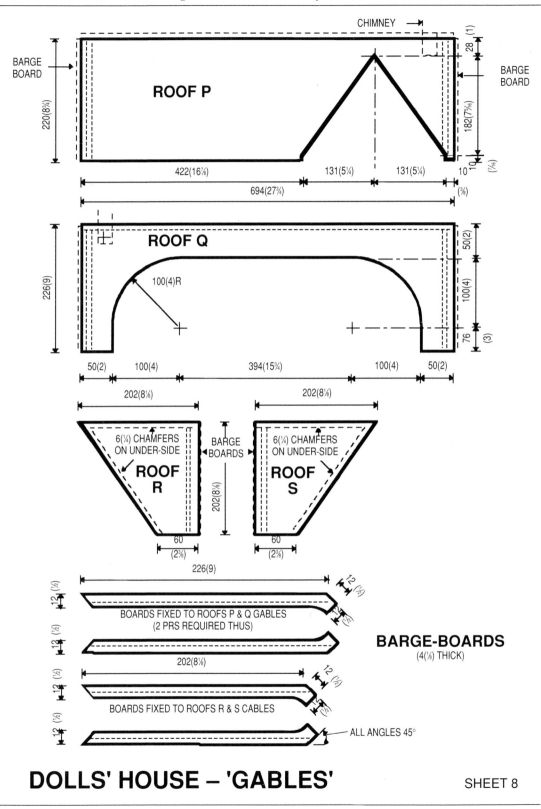

ROOF P

BARGE BOARD

CHIMNEY

BARGE BOARD

220(8¾)

28 (1)

182(7⁷⁄₁₆)

422(16⅞)

131(5¼)

131(5¼)

10 (⅜)

694(27¾)

ROOF Q

226(9)

100(4)R

50(2)

100(4)

76 (3)

50(2)   100(4)   394(15¾)   100(4)   50(2)

202(8⅛)   202(8⅛)

6(¼) CHAMFERS ON UNDER-SIDE

BARGE BOARDS

6(¼) CHAMFERS ON UNDER-SIDE

ROOF R

ROOF S

202(8⅛)

60 (2⅜)   60 (2⅜)

226(9)

12 (½)

12 (½)

BOARDS FIXED TO ROOFS P & Q GABLES
(2 PRS REQUIRED THUS)

12 (½)

12 (½)

BARGE-BOARDS
(4(⅛) THICK)

202(8⅛)

12 (½)

12 (½)

12 (½)

BOARDS FIXED TO ROOFS R & S GABLES

12 (½)

ALL ANGLES 45°

DOLLS' HOUSE – 'GABLES'

SHEET 8

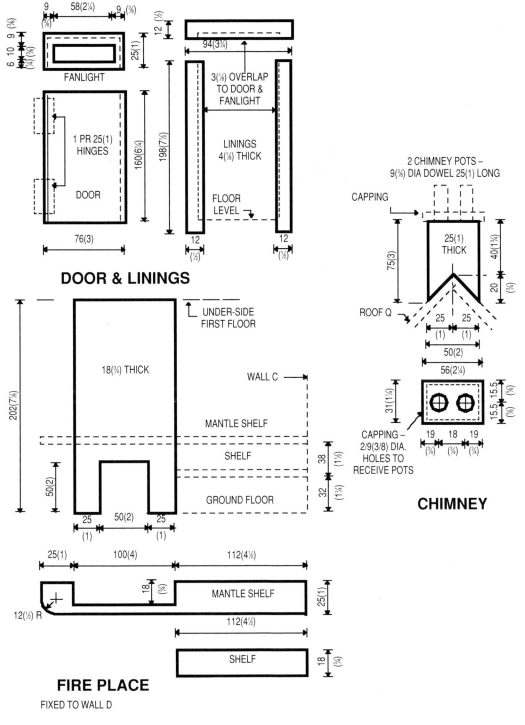

DOOR & LININGS

FANLIGHT

1 PR 25(1) HINGES

DOOR

3(⅛) OVERLAP TO DOOR & FANLIGHT

LININGS 4(⅛) THICK

FLOOR LEVEL

2 CHIMNEY POTS – 9(⅜) DIA DOWEL 25(1) LONG

CAPPING

25(1) THICK

ROOF Q

CHIMNEY

CAPPING – 2/9(3/8) DIA. HOLES TO RECEIVE POTS

UNDER-SIDE FIRST FLOOR

18(¾) THICK

WALL C

MANTLE SHELF

SHELF

GROUND FLOOR

MANTLE SHELF

12(½) R

FIRE PLACE

FIXED TO WALL D

SHELF

DOLLS' HOUSE – 'GABLES'

SHEET 9

77

PROJECT 6

A ZOO

W ith the design of this toy an attempt has been made to produce an interesting layout which makes the toy that much more fun for a child to play with. The viewing walkways with the flight of steps and ramped access also incorporate a hinged roof over the cages which provides easier access to them.

The scale will suit the size of the toy animals sold in the majority of toy shops and is approximately 1/24 ($\frac{1}{2}$ inch to the foot).

CUTTING LIST

498 × 498 × 4 mm (20 × 20 × $\frac{1}{8}$ in)   plywood or hardboard

1000 × 800 × 6 mm (40 × 32 × $\frac{1}{4}$ in)   plywood

100 × 100 × 4 mm (4 × 4 × $\frac{1}{8}$ in)   plywood

250 × 112 × 12 mm (9$\frac{1}{2}$ × 4$\frac{1}{2}$ × $\frac{1}{2}$ in)   timber

312 × 15 × 9 mm (12$\frac{1}{2}$ × $\frac{5}{8}$ × $\frac{3}{8}$ in)   timber

6 × 6 × 1240 mm ($\frac{1}{4}$ × $\frac{1}{4}$ × 49 in)   timber fillet

5 mm × ($\frac{3}{16}$ in) diameter × 1392 mm (52 in)   timber dowel

ANCILLARIES

1 pair 25 mm (1 in) brass hinges

1 small knob

CONSTRUCTION DETAILS

1. Mark and cut out the 4 mm ($\frac{1}{8}$ in) thick base and mark on it the locations of the walls as illustrated on the plans.

2. Mark and cut the components to form walls A, B, C, D, E, F, G, H, J, K, L, M, and N.

3. Cut from the 12 mm ($\frac{1}{2}$ in) thick timber two long (115 mm [4$\frac{1}{2}$ in] and two short (65 mm (2$\frac{1}{2}$ in)) 12 × 12 mm ($\frac{1}{2}$ × $\frac{1}{2}$ in) posts.

4. Cut out the pieces to make the flight of steps, i.e. the two sides, the base, piece Z and the six treads. Assemble the steps as follows:

   i. Glue and pin a side to each long edge of the base.

  ii. Glue and pin piece Z to the base and to the vertical end edges of the sides.

 iii. Glue the treads onto the stepped top edges of the sides commencing with the bottom tread.

Lay the completed assembly of the steps aside to allow the glue to achieve its full bond.

5. Glue and pin a long and a short post to the ends of wall A ensuring that a 6 mm ($\frac{1}{4}$ in) space is left between the posts and the end edges of the wall to accommodate the adjoining walls.

Glue and pin two lengths of 6 × 6 mm ($\frac{1}{4}$ × $\frac{1}{4}$ in) fillet to wall A in the correct position to support the walkway Q and located between walls E–F, and wall F–piece Z (on the flight of steps) where these will abut wall A.

Glue and pin the flight of steps assembly to wall A so that its base is flush with the base of the wall and piece Z is located in its correct position against the wall.

6. Mark the line of the top surface of the ramp on wall B by reference to the dimensions given on the plans. Glue and pin a length of 6 × 6 mm ($\frac{1}{4}$ × $\frac{1}{4}$ in) fillet to the wall so that it is 6 mm ($\frac{1}{4}$ in) below the ramp line previously marked. This fillet will support the ramp.

7. Glue and pin a long and a short post to the ends of wall C ensuring that a 6 mm ($\frac{1}{4}$ in) space is left between the posts and the end edges of the wall to accommodate the adjoining walls.

8. Fix wall A to wall B by glueing and pinning through wall A into the edge of wall B, and through wall B into the post previously fixed to wall A.

9. Fix wall D to wall A by glueing and pinning in a similar manner to that described in instruction 8.

10. Fix wall C to walls B and D by glueing and pinning through wall C into the edges of walls B and D, and through walls B and D into the posts previously fixed to wall C. Ensure that the completed assembly of walls A, B, C and D is square and sits level, and set it aside to allow the glued joints to achieve a full bond.

11. Cut out piece E1 and glue and pin it to wall E ensuring that its top edge is flush with what will be the top surface of the cage roof. The ends of piece E1 will abut walls G and K, and the notches cut into the piece will accommodate the top ends of walls H and J. Cut the recesses to receive hinges in piece E1 at this stage.

12. Glue and pin wall J to wall E in its correct position with a top edge located in the appropriate notch cut in piece E1.

13. Glue the contact edges of the joint to be formed by sliding the slots cut in walls E and H into each other. Assemble the joint ensuring that the walls are squared to each other.

14. Cut out the pieces F1 and F2 and the 16 lengths of dowel to form the cage bars. Drill the 5 mm ($\frac{3}{16}$ in) diameter holes in pieces F1 and F2 to receive the bars. It is recommended that this be done by taping the two pieces together in their correct relative positions and to drill down through piece F2 into F1 with the drill bit marked to indicate when it has reached its correct depth of 6 mm ($\frac{1}{4}$ in) into F1. This process will ensure that the bars will be correctly aligned.

15. Fix the bars to wall F as follows:

i.   Glue and pin piece F2 into its correct position on the base of wall F with the sides of the wall openings fitting into the notches cut out of piece F2.

ii.   Fit a piece of dowel (cut to the correct length) into each hole drilled for this purpose in piece F2.

iii. Locate the top ends of the dowels into the holes drilled into piece F1 and glue and pin

this piece to wall F with its top edge flush with the line of the underside of the cage roof.

16. Cut out the cage roof P component. Glue and pin two lengths of 6 × 6 mm ($\frac{1}{4}$ × $\frac{1}{4}$ in) fillet to its underside along one edge, so that they will be located between the tops of walls A–H and J–K when the roof is in its required position on the cages. Cut recesses for the hinges in the edge of the roof/fillet to coincide with the recesses previously cut in piece E1 for this same purpose. Secure the two hinges in the recesses on the roof piece..

Fix the small knob to the top surface of the roof P.

17. With wall F held in its correct position against walls H and J check that the roof will fit neatly in its required position with its hinged edge against piece E1 on wall E, and the other edge resting on the top edge of piece F1 fixed to wall F. Trim the shape of roof P as necessary to achieve this fit and when satisfied, screw the hinges to piece E1 to secure the roof. (Note that it is more convenient to secure the hinged roof at this stage than to fix it at a later stage of assembly.)

18. Glue and pin wall F to walls H and J. Note that the cut-outs in walls H and J should fit around pieces F1 and F2 which are fixed to wall F.

19. Glue the contact edges of the joint to be formed by sliding the slots cut in walls F and G into each other. Glue the contact edge of wall G where it abuts wall E. Assemble wall F into wall G and pin through wall E into the edge of wall G.

20. Fix the assembly of walls E, F, G, H and J into their position within the assembly of walls

A, B, C and D by glueing the contact edges and pinning through wall A into the edges of walls E and F; through wall D into the edge of wall H; through wall C into the edge of wall E; and through wall G into the side of the steps assembly previously fixed to wall A. This and similar future operations should be carried out with the whole assembly seated firmly on a level base.

21. Glue and pin lengths of 6 × 6 mm ($\frac{1}{4}$ × $\frac{1}{4}$ in) fillet to wall K so that their tops will align with the underside of walkway R and be located between walls E – piece F1 on wall F; F–M; M–N; and N–B as illustrated on the plans.

22. Glue the contact edges of the joint to be formed by sliding the slots cut in walls K and M into each other and assemble this joint ensuring that the walls are squared to each other.

23. Fix the assembly of walls K and M into the assembly previously completed (*see instruction 20*) by glueing and pinning through wall E into the edge of wall K; through wall B into the edge of wall K; through wall C into the edge of wall M; and through wall K into the edge of wall F.

24. Glue and pin a length of 6 × 6 mm ($\frac{1}{4}$ × $\frac{1}{4}$ in) fillet to wall L so that its top will align with the underside of walkway R and with it located between walls M–N.

25. Glue and pin a length of 6 × 6 mm ($\frac{1}{4}$ × $\frac{1}{4}$ in) fillet to wall N so that its top edge will align with the underside of ramp S, all as described for the similar fillet fixing to wall B (instruction 6).

26. Glue the contact edges of the joint to be formed by sliding the slots cut in walls L and N into each other and assemble this joint ensuring that the walls are squared to each other.

27. Fix the assembly of walls L and N into the assembly previously completed (*instruction 23*) by glueing and pinning through wall L into the edge of wall M; through wall B into the edge of wall L; through wall K into the edge of wall N; and through wall F into the parapet edge of wall L.

28. Cut out the components to form the walkways Q and R, and ramp S.

29. Glue and fix walkway Q into its position seated on the fillets previously fixed to walls A and G. Pin through these walls into the walkway edges and down through the walkway into the top of wall G.

30. Glue and fix walkway R into its position seated on the fillets previously fixed to walls K and L. Pin through these walls into the walkway edges and down through the walkway into the top of wall L.

31. Cut the chamfers on the underside of each end of the ramp S. Glue and fix it into its position seated on the fillets previously fixed to walls B and N. Pin through these walls into the ramp edges to secure it.

This is an opportune time to paint or varnish the completed assembly of the walls, and also the base, before final assembly. The walls of the toy portrayed in the photograph have been varnished, and the surface of the walkways, ramp and cage roof have been finished with a 'crazy-paving' patterned paper. The base has been finished with a blue paint to represent water in the area bounded by walls M–C–B–N–piece T. The other animal enclosure floors have been finished with a green flock paper; varnish inside the cages and office; and the remainder of the base with a 'crazy-paving' patterned paper.

32. Place the finished assembly of walls on the base and confirm the locations of screw-fixings into the bottoms of the four posts and into piece F2. After drilling holes for the screws (*see Section 2*) glue the bottom edges of the wall assembly and secure it to the base using 4 no $\frac{5}{8}$ in × 4 countersunk (c/s) screws into the bottoms of the 12 × 12 mm ($\frac{1}{2}$ × $\frac{1}{2}$ in) posts and 2 No $\frac{1}{4}$ in × 4 c/s screws into piece F2.

33. Cut out the pieces (representing rocks) T and U (6 mm ($\frac{1}{4}$ in) thick) and V, W and X (12 mm ($\frac{1}{2}$ in) thick). The shape of piece U is arbitrary so long as it will fit onto piece T, as is the curved shape on each of the other pieces T, V, W and X, so long as the critical dimensions as shown on the plans are maintained.

34. Glue and pin piece U onto piece T. Varnish or paint this assembly. Glue and pin it onto the base abutting walls L and N.

35. Glue and pin piece W onto piece V. Varnish or paint this assembly. Glue it into position on the base against walls B–C–K with the corner notch accommodating the post fixed into the corner of walls B and C.

36. Varnish or paint piece X. Glue it into position on the base against walls A–D–E with the corner notch accommodating the post fixed into the corner of walls A and D.

37. Complete the toy by cutting the 'ZOO' motif out of 4 mm ($\frac{1}{8}$ in) thick plywood and glue and pin it to the outside face of wall A in line with the window which is cut in this wall. (If preferred this instruction can be carried out at an earlier stage – possibly with instruction 5.)

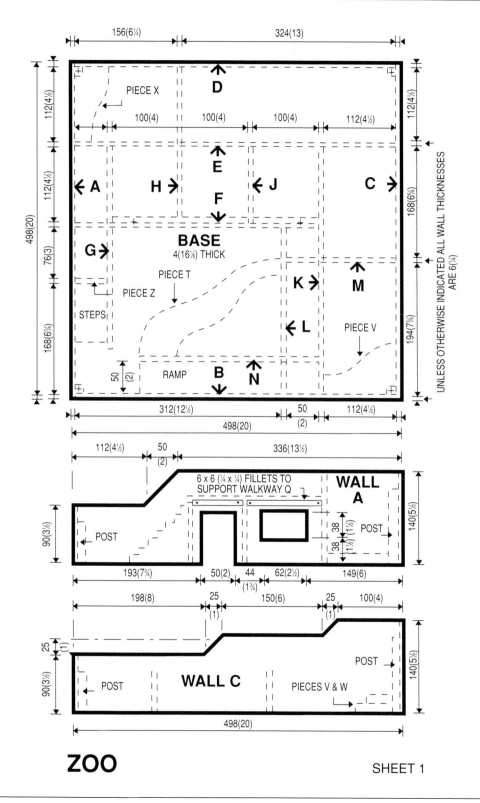

156(6¼) 324(13)

112(4½)

PIECE X

100(4) 100(4) 100(4) 112(4½)

112(4½) D

498(20) ←A H→ E ←J C→ 112(4½)

F 168(6¾)

76(3) G→ **BASE**
4(16⅛) THICK

PIECE T

PIECE Z K→ M

168(6¾) STEPS L← PIECE V

194(7¾)

50
(2) RAMP B N

312(12½) 50 112(4½)
(2)

498(20)

UNLESS OTHERWISE INDICATED ALL WALL THICKNESSES ARE 6(¼)

112(4½) 50 336(13½)
(2)

6 x 6 (¼ x ¼) FILLETS TO
SUPPORT WALKWAY Q **WALL
A**

90(3½) POST 38 140(5½)
38 POST
(1½)
(1½)

193(7¾) 50(2) 44 62(2½) 149(6)
(1¾)

198(8) 25 150(6) 25 100(4)
(1) (1)

25 POST
(1)

90(3½) POST **WALL C** PIECES V & W 140(5½)

498(20)

ZOO

SHEET 1

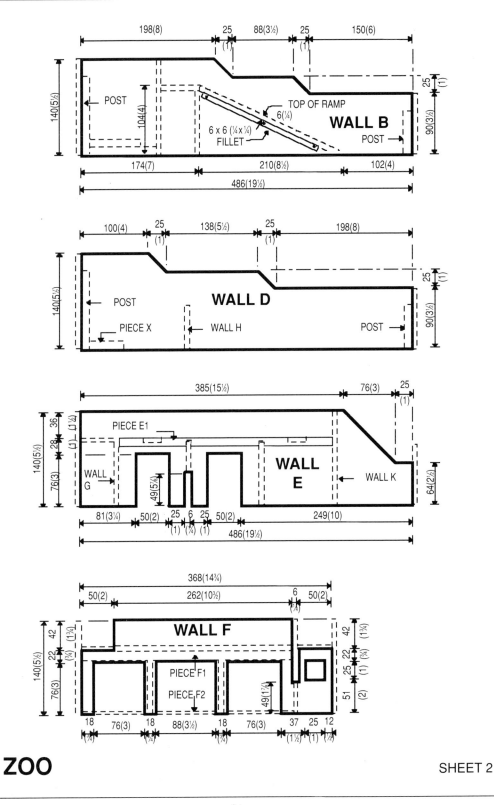

ZOO

SHEET 2

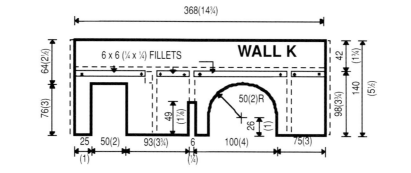

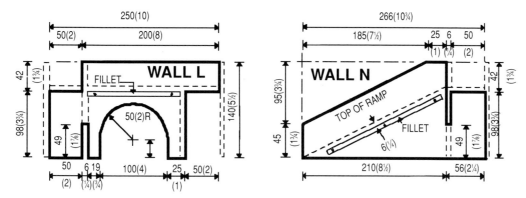

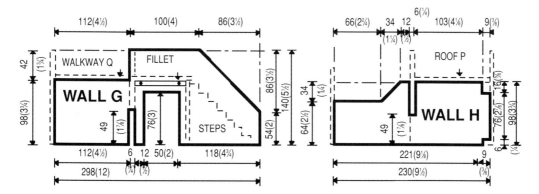

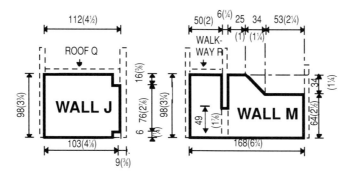

ZOO

SHEET 3

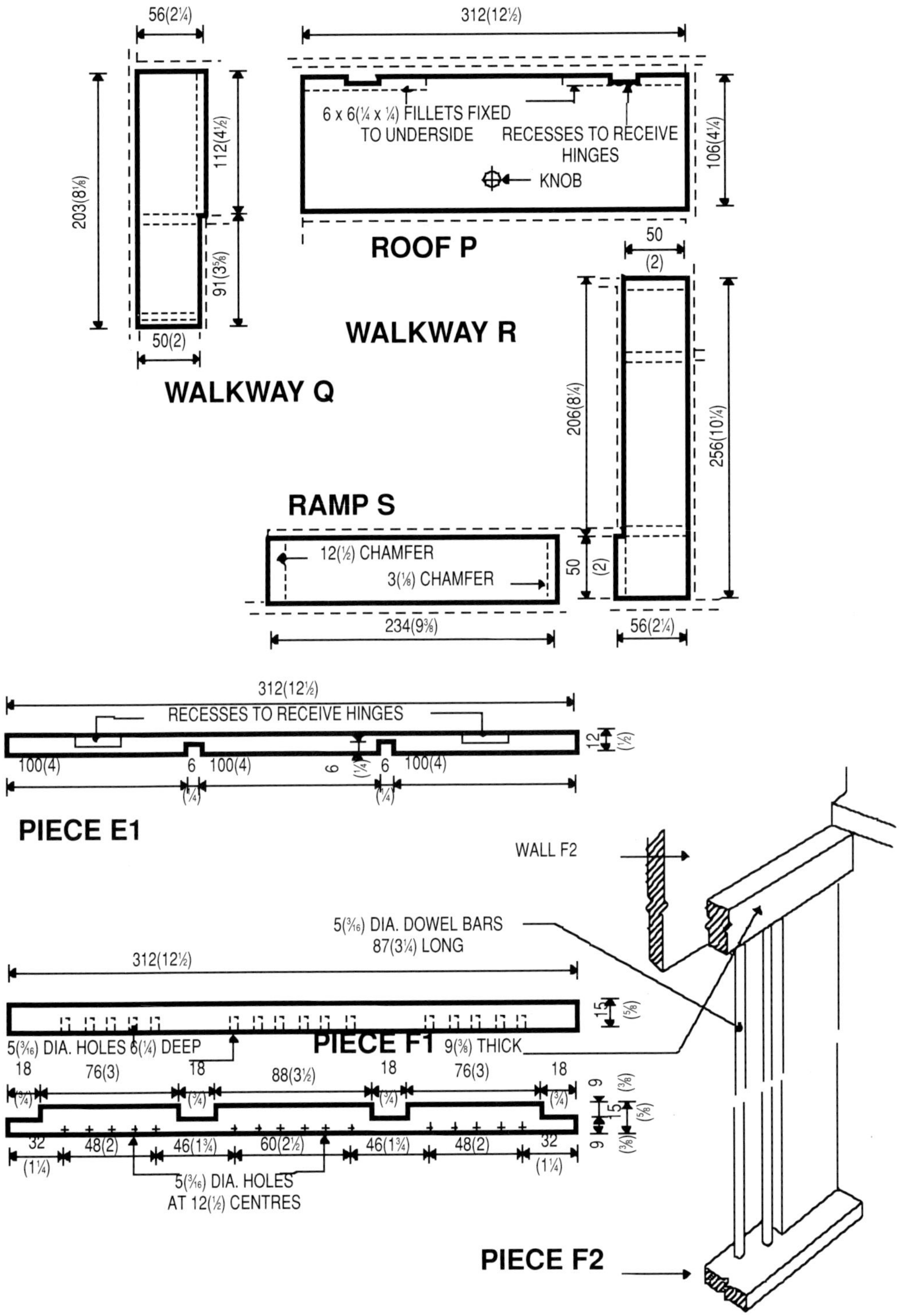
56(2¼)
203(8⅛)
112(4½)
91(3⅝)
50(2)
WALKWAY Q
312(12½)
6 x 6(¼ x ¼) FILLETS FIXED TO UNDERSIDE
RECESSES TO RECEIVE HINGES
KNOB
106(4¼)
ROOF P
WALKWAY R
50 (2)
206(8¼)
256(10¼)
RAMP S
12(½) CHAMFER
3(⅛) CHAMFER
234(9⅜)
50 (2)
56(2¼)
312(12½)
RECESSES TO RECEIVE HINGES
12 (½)
100(4)
6 (¼)
100(4)
6 (¼)
100(4)
PIECE E1
WALL F2
5(3/16) DIA. DOWEL BARS 87(3¼) LONG
312(12½)
15 (⅝)
5(3/16) DIA. HOLES 6(¼) DEEP
PIECE F1
9(⅜) THICK
18 (¾)
76(3)
18 (¾)
88(3½)
18 (¾)
76(3)
18 (¾)
9 (⅜)
15 (⅝)
9 (⅜)
32 (1¼)
48(2)
46(1¾)
60(2½)
46(1¾)
48(2)
32 (1¼)
5(3/16) DIA. HOLES AT 12(½) CENTRES
PIECE F2

ZOO

SHEET 4

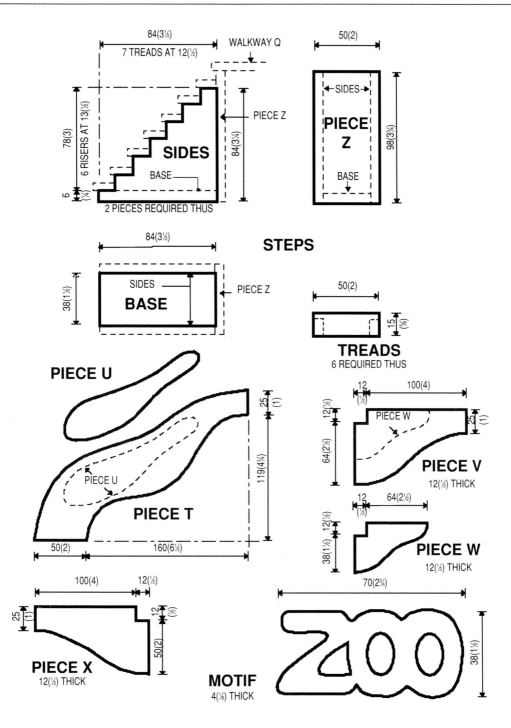

84(3½)

7 TREADS AT 12(½)

WALKWAY Q

PIECE Z

78(3)

6 RISERS AT 13(½)

84(3¼)

SIDES

BASE

6 (¼)

2 PIECES REQUIRED THUS

50(2)

←SIDES→

PIECE Z

98(3¾)

BASE

STEPS

84(3½)

SIDES

BASE

PIECE Z

38(1½)

50(2)

15 (⅝)

TREADS
6 REQUIRED THUS

PIECE U

25 (1)

119(4¾)

PIECE U

PIECE T

50(2)   160(6½)

12 (½)   100(4)

12(½)

PIECE W

25 (1)

64(2½)

PIECE V
12(½) THICK

12 (½)   64(2½)

38(1½)   12(½)

PIECE W
12(½) THICK

100(4)   12(½)

25 (1)

12 (½)

50(2)

70(2¾)

PIECE X
12(½) THICK

MOTIF
4(⅛) THICK

38(1½)

PROJECT 7

'BAY WINDOWS' DOLLS' HOUSE

The design of this house is based on a North American 'frontier' house with its balcony and gable bay windows being a distinctive feature.

The roofs of the house illustrated in the photograph have been finished with cedar shingles which enhance its appearance, but these are an optional extra and need not be added if availability should prove to be a problem.

The scale of this toy is 1/12 (1 inch to 1 foot).

CUTTING LIST

700 × 375 × 12 mm (28 × 15 × $\frac{1}{2}$ in)	plywood
2400 × 1200 × 6 mm (96 × 48 × $\frac{1}{4}$ in)	plywood
360 × 250 × 4 mm (14 × 10 × $\frac{1}{8}$ in)	plywood
730 × 100 × 12 mm (29 × 4 × $\frac{1}{2}$ in)	timber
12 mm ($\frac{1}{2}$ in) diameter × 76 mm (3 in)	timber dowel
6 mm × ($\frac{1}{4}$ in) diameter × 24 mm (1 in)	timber dowel
6 × 6 × 2060 mm ($\frac{1}{4}$ × $\frac{1}{4}$ × 90 in)	timber fillet

ANCILLARIES

2 pairs 25 mm (1 in) brass hinges

CONSTRUCTION DETAILS

1. Mark and cut out the base (12 mm ($\frac{1}{2}$ in) thick), the first and attic floors, walls A, B, C, D, E, F, J, K and L, and piece M.

2. Complete the cutting of the windows (2 No type W1; 4 No type W2; 3 No type W3; 2 No type W4) using the pieces cut from walls C, D, E, F and J, and piece M to form their openings (*as described in Section 2*). Paint or stain these items and put them aside to dry.

3. Complete the cutting of the two doors using the pieces cut from wall J to form their openings. Paint or stain these items and put them aside to dry.

4. Cut the 3 mm ($\frac{1}{8}$ in) chamfer along the front edge of wall A.

Cut out the fireplace piece (12 mm ($\frac{1}{2}$ in) thick) and glue and pin this to the inside face of wall A ensuring that a 12 mm ($\frac{1}{2}$ in) space is left between the bottom of the fireplace and the bottom edge of the wall to accommodate the base to which this wall will be fixed.

Glue and pin lengths of 6 × 6 mm ($\frac{1}{4}$ × $\frac{1}{4}$ in) fillet to the inside face of wall A to provide supports for the first and attic floors. Ensure that the top fillet leaves a 6 mm ($\frac{1}{4}$ in) space at the back edge to accommodate piece M when it is fixed.

5. Cut the 3 mm ($\frac{1}{8}$ in) chamfer along the front edge of wall B.

Fix a length of 6 × 6 mm ($\frac{1}{4}$ × $\frac{1}{4}$ in) fillet to the balcony side face of wall B where it will abut piece H. The top end of this fillet should terminate at the underside of the balcony floor at the first floor level.

6. Cut the 3 mm ($\frac{1}{8}$ in) chamfers along the two edges of wall C.

Fix a length of 6 × 6 mm ($\frac{1}{4}$ × $\frac{1}{4}$ in) fillet to the inside face of wall C to provide support for the first floor.

7. Cut the 3 mm ($\frac{1}{8}$ in) chamfers along the two edges of both walls D and E.

8. Fix a length of 6 × 6 mm ($\frac{1}{4}$ × $\frac{1}{4}$ in) fillet to the inside face of wall F to provide support for the attic floor. Ensure that a 6 mm ($\frac{1}{4}$ in) space is

left at the back edge to accommodate piece M when it is fixed.

9. Cut out the six window shutters from 4 mm ($\frac{1}{8}$ in) thick plywood. Paint or stain these items and allow them to dry.

Glue and pin a shutter to each side of the two window openings on the outside face of wall J.

10. Glue the windows (completed at instruction 2) back into the openings from which they were originally cut in walls C, D, E, F and J, and piece M.

11. Cut out the two door frames and glue and pin them to the outside face of wall J so that they overhang the door openings by 3 mm ($\frac{1}{8}$ in).

Also fix a length of 6 × 6 mm ($\frac{1}{4}$ × $\frac{1}{4}$ in) fillet to the outside face of wall J to provide support for the balcony floor.

12. Fix one pair of 25 mm (1 in) hinges to the backs of the two doors. Also fix a door knob to the front and back of each door (knobs made as described in Project 10, Corner Shop, from 6 mm ($\frac{1}{4}$ in) diameter dowel)

Fix the doors into their openings in wall J by securing the hinges to the wall so that the doors open inwards. When closed they should neatly fit into the rebates formed by the overhang of the door frames around the door openings. Note that a clearance of 6 mm ($\frac{1}{4}$ in) should be left below the upper door to accommodate the first floor when it is fixed.

13. Cut out the pieces to make the stair, i.e. sides P and Q; back R; base S; and the treads and risers (4 mm ($\frac{1}{8}$ in) thick). Construct the stair as follows:

i.   Glue and pin the back R to an end of the base S.

ii.   Glue and pin the sides P and Q to the edges of the assembled base S and back R.

iii. Glue the treads and risers onto the 'steps' cut in the sides P and Q, commencing with the bottom riser, then the bottom tread, the second riser, *et seq*, finishing with the 10 mm ($\frac{3}{8}$ in) high top riser.

14. Glue and pin the assembled stair to the face of wall L so that the vertical back edge of the stair aligns with the edge of wall L where it will abut wall F. The door opening cut in the stair side Q should align with the opening cut in wall L.

15. Glue the edge of wall K where it will abut wall L and secure it in its position by pining through wall L into the edge of wall K. This and the following two instructions should be carried out with the components seated on a firm, level base.

16. Fix wall J to the assembly of walls K, L and the stair by glueing and pinning throgh wall J into the side of the stair and into the edge of wall K where it adjoins wall J above the first floor level.

17. Glue and pin wall F into its position against the back of the assembly of the stair and wall L. Pin through wall J into the edge of wall F.

18. Check that the first floor will slide with its slots into the slots cut in walls K and F so that the floor abuts the inside face of wall J with the stair landing projection on the floor in place at the top of the stair and the doorway projection fitting into the upper doorway below the door. When satisfied that the fit is correct glue the joint and wall contact edges and slide the floor back into its position. Pin through wall J into the edges of the floor where they abut this wall.

19. Glue the joint and wall contact edges on wall B and slide the slot cut in this wall into the appropriate slot cut in the first floor. When pushed firmly into its correct position, pin through wall B into the edge of wall J.

This is an opportune time to apply the required finishes to the assembly of walls B, K, F, J and L with the stair and first floor, and to the base and inside faces of walls A, C, D and E, and to the underside of the attic floor, taking care to keep the finish material off the surfaces which are to make glued contact with other components.

20. Glue the bottom contact edges of the assembly of walls B, F, K, J and L with the stair and first floor and locate it in its correct position on the base. Note that the small projection at the bottom front edge of wall B will locate over the edge of the base against where it projects 6 mm ($\frac{1}{4}$ in) at the side of the bay window projection. Screw through the base into the bottom of the stair using a $\frac{3}{4}$ in × 6 countersunk (c/s) screw, and pin through the base into the bottom edges of walls B, K and F.

21. Glue and screw wall A to the base using 2 No $\frac{5}{8}$ in × 4 c/s screws, and pin through the wall into the edge of the first floor which should be seated on the fillets previously fixed to this wall for this purpose.

22. Glue the joint and contact edges of the attic floor and slide the slot cut in it into the slot cut in the top of the wall B so that the floor is located in its correct position seated on the fillets previously fixed to walls A and F, and abutting wall J. Pin through walls A, F and J into the edges of the attic floor and pin through the floor into the top edge of wall K.

23. Cut out the piece N and glue and pin it to the underside of the attic floor where it will provide edges against which the tops of walls D and E will abut and be fixed to form the bay window.

24. Glue and screw wall C to the base using a $\frac{5}{8}$ in × 4 c/s screw, and pin through the wall into the edges of the first and attic floors where they adjoin this wall.

25. Check that wall D fits neatly into its position with its chamfered edges abutting the chamfers cut on the edges of the adjoining walls A and C. When satisfied, glue and screw this wall to the base using a $\frac{5}{8}$ in × 4 c/s screw and pin through it into the edges of the first floor and piece N (fixed to the underside of the attic floor).

26. Repeat instruction 25 to fix wall E into its position adjoining walls B and C.

27. Glue piece M into its position at the back and against the edge of the attic floor, and

located in the checks cut out of the top edges of walls B and K. Pin through piece M into the edge of the attic floor and pin into its end edges through walls A and F.

28. Cut out the pieces G and H components. Complete the cutting of the balustrades using the pieces cut from G and H for this purpose. Cut out the balustrade cappings. Paint or stain the balustrades and their cappings as required and put them aside to dry.

29. Fix 6 × 6 mm ($\frac{1}{4}$ × $\frac{1}{4}$ in) fillets to pieces G and H to provide support to the balcony floor.

30. Glue and screw piece H to the base using 3 No $\frac{5}{8}$ in × 4 c/s screws. One end of this piece will be located against the fillet previously fixed to the wall B. Pin through wall B into the edge of piece H and pin through piece H into the edge of the first floor where it abuts its balcony projection.

31. Glue and screw piece G to the base using 2 No $\frac{5}{8}$ in × 4 c/s screws. Pin through it into the edge of the first floor (which will be seated on the fillet previously fixed to piece G for this purpose). Pin through piece H into the edge of piece G.

32. Cut out the separate balcony floor piece. Apply glue to the fillets previously fixed to wall J and piece H onto which this piece of balcony floor can now be seated.

33. Glue and fix the balcony balustrades back into the locations from which these pieces were originally cut from pieces G and H.

Glue and fix a balustrade capping piece onto each balustrade with the cut-outs at each end slotted into the 'posts' on pieces G and H between which the balustrades are located.

34. Mark and cut out the components for roofs T, U, V and W.

35. Glue and pin roof T onto the wall A side of the gables on wall C, and piece M. Ensure that this roof projects equally 6 mm ($\frac{1}{4}$ in) beyond the gables at each end.

36. Check that roof U fits onto the other side of roof T with the cut-out on its base giving clearance for the upstand gable on wall B. When satisfied, glue and pin roof U onto its position on the gables on wall C and piece M. Pin through roof U into the edge of roof T where it abuts it along the length of the ridge.

37. Cut out the truss X component. Cut the chamfer on the inclined edge of roof W. Glue and pin the truss X to the underside of the roof W so that it is located 6 mm ($\frac{1}{4}$ in) from the roof's gable edge and with its apex flush with the top edge of the roof W.

38. Check that the roof W (with truss X) fits properly in its position on the back edges of the gables on walls B and F and with its chamfered edge fitting neatly against the slope of roof U. When satisfied, glue and pin roof W into its position.

39. Cut the chamfer on the inclined edge of the roof V and check that it fits properly in its position on the front edges of the gables on walls B and F and on the edge of the truss X previously fixed to the roof W, and with the chamfered edge fitting neatly against the slope of roof U. When satisfied, glue and pin roof V into

its position on these components and pin through it into the edge of roof W where it abuts it along the length of the ridge.

40. Cut out the components to make the chimney, i.e. the long and the short lengths of 12 mm ($\frac{1}{2}$ in) thick stack; the capping piece; and the two pieces of 12 mm ($\frac{1}{2}$ in) diameter dowel chimney pots.

Glue and pin the short length of stack to the top of the longer piece. Glue and pin this stack assembly to the outside face of wall A with the thickened top fitting into the notch cut out of roof T to accommodate it.

Glue and pin the chimney capping piece onto the top of the stack. Glue and fit the two dowel pots into the holes cut in the capping piece.

41. Cut out the six components to make the barge boards. Glue and pin a pair of the longer boards to each end of the roofs T and U at their gables over wall C and piece M. Glue and pin the pair of the shorter boards to the ends of the roofs V and W at their gable over the truss X.

42. If the roofs are to be tiled, these can now be fixed commencing with the bottom rows and working up towards the ridge on each roof slope. Finish the ridges with a length of 12 × 2 mm ($\frac{1}{2}$ × $\frac{1}{16}$ in) strip fixed to each side. This ridge finish should be fixed whatever finish is chosen for the roofs.

43. Complete the house by applying the desired external finishes.

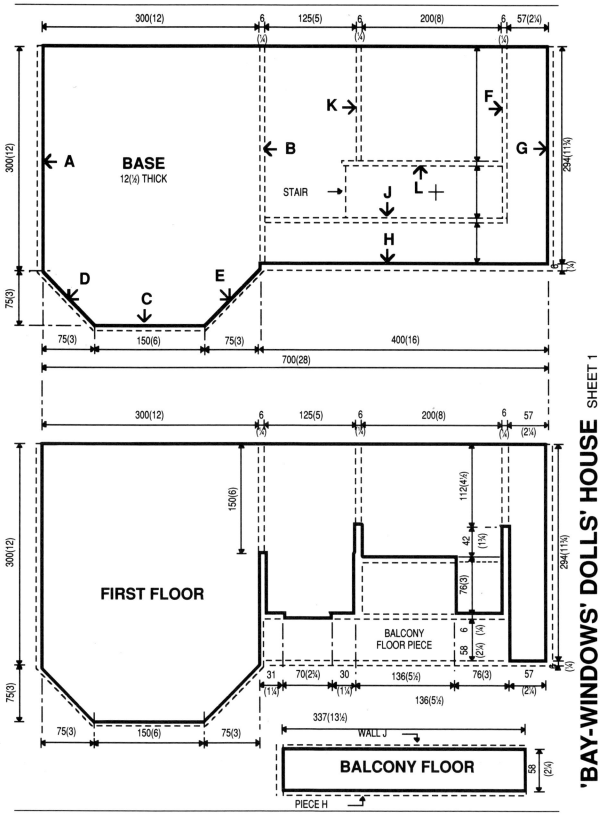

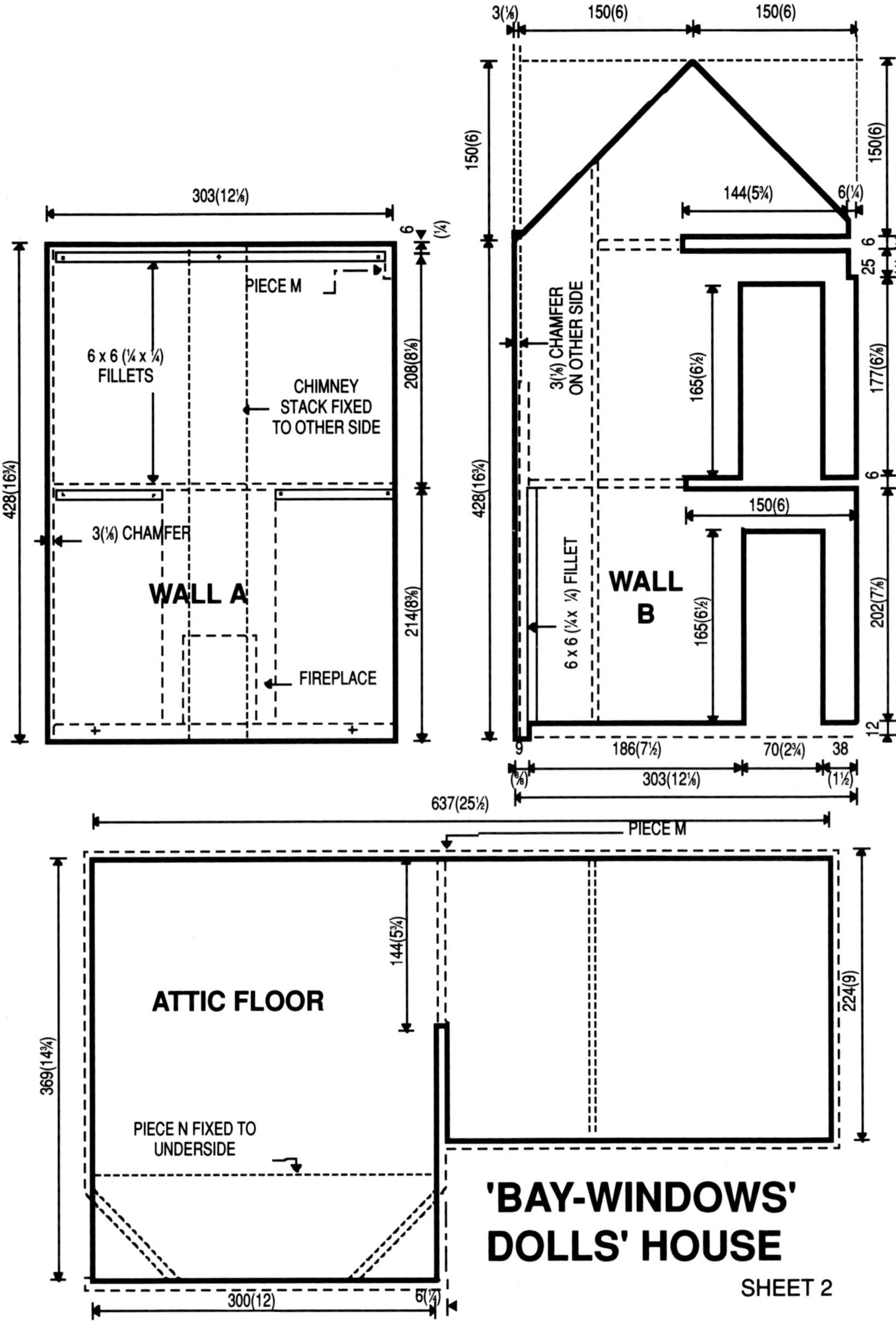
303(12⅛)
6 (¼)
PIECE M
6 x 6 (¼ x ¼) FILLETS
CHIMNEY STACK FIXED TO OTHER SIDE
208(8⅛)
428(16¾)
3(⅛) CHAMFER
WALL A
214(8⅜)
FIREPLACE
3(⅛)
150(6)
150(6)
150(6)
150(6)
144(5¾)
6(¼)
6 (¼)
25 (1)
3(⅛) CHAMFER ON OTHER SIDE
165(6½)
177(6⅞)
428(16¾)
6 (¼)
150(6)
6 x 6 (¼ x ¼) FILLET
WALL B
165(6½)
202(7⅞)
12 (½)
9 (⅜)
186(7½)
70(2¾)
38 (1½)
303(12⅛)
637(25½)
PIECE M
144(5¾)
ATTIC FLOOR
224(9)
369(14¾)
PIECE N FIXED TO UNDERSIDE
300(12)
6(¼)
'BAY-WINDOWS' DOLLS' HOUSE
SHEET 2

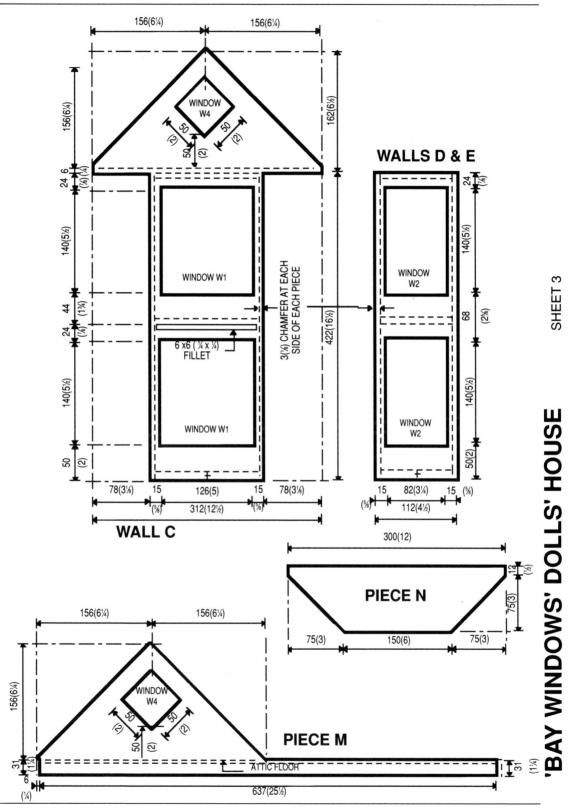

WALLS D & E

WINDOW W4

50 (2) 50 (2) 50 (2)

156(6¼) 156(6¼)

162(6½)

WINDOW W1

140(5½)

3(⅛) CHAMFER AT EACH SIDE OF EACH PIECE

422(16½)

6 x6 (¼ x ¼)
FILLET

24 6 (⁷⁄₈) (¼)

44 (1¾)

24 (⁷⁄₈)

140(5½)

WINDOW W1

50 (2)

78(3⅛) 15 (⁵⁄₈) 126(5) 15 (⁵⁄₈) 78(3⅛)

312(12½)

WALL C

WINDOW W2

24 (⁷⁄₈)

140(5½)

68 (2⅝)

140(5½)

50(2)

WINDOW W2

15 82(3¼) 15 (⁵⁄₈)

(⁵⁄₈) 112(4½)

300(12)

PIECE N

12 (½)

75(3)

75(3) 150(6) 75(3)

156(6¼) 156(6¼)

156(6¼)

WINDOW W4

50 (2) 50 (2)

50 (2)

PIECE M

31 (1¼)

ATTIC FLOOR

31 (1¼)

6 (¼)

637(25½)

SHEET 3

'BAY WINDOWS' DOLLS' HOUSE

95

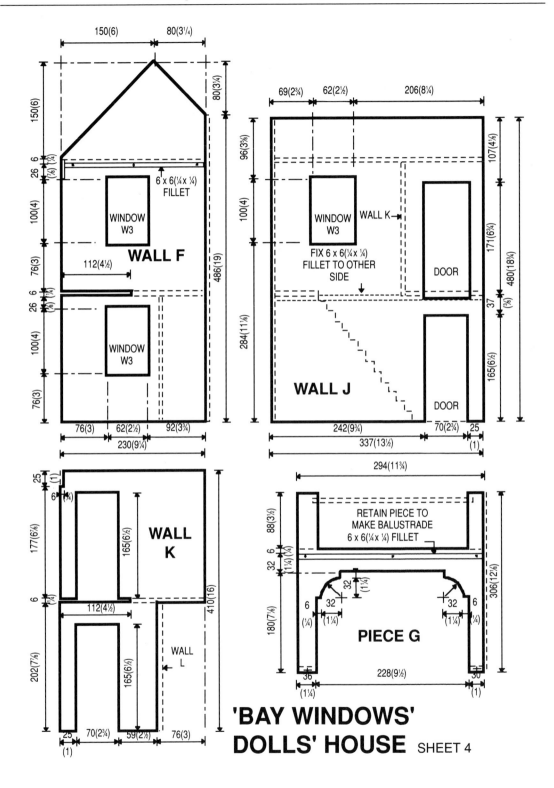

WALL F

150(6)   80(3¼)

150(6)

80(3¾)

26   6(⅛)(¼)

6 x 6(¼ x ¼) FILLET

100(4)

WINDOW W3

76(3)

112(4½)

26   6(⅛)(¼)

486(19)

100(4)

WINDOW W3

76(3)

76(3)   62(2½)   92(3¾)

230(9¼)

WALL J

69(2¾)   62(2½)   206(8¼)

96(3¾)

100(4)

WINDOW W3

WALL K

FIX 6 x 6(¼ x ¼) FILLET TO OTHER SIDE

DOOR

107(4⅛)

171(6¾)

480(18¾)

37(3⁄8)

DOOR

165(6½)

284(11⅛)

242(9¾)   70(2¾)   25(1)

337(13½)

WALL K

25(1)

6(¼)

177(6¾)

165(6½)

WALL K

6(¼)

112(4½)

202(7⅞)

165(6½)

WALL L

410(16)

25(1)   70(2¾)   59(2½)   76(3)

PIECE G

294(11¾)

88(3½)

RETAIN PIECE TO MAKE BALUSTRADE
6 x 6(¼ x ¼) FILLET

32   6(1¼)(¼)

32(1¼)

6(¼)   32(1¼)   32(1¼)   6(¼)

180(7⅞)

306(12⅛)

36(1¼)   228(9½)   30(1)

'BAY WINDOWS'
DOLLS' HOUSE SHEET 4

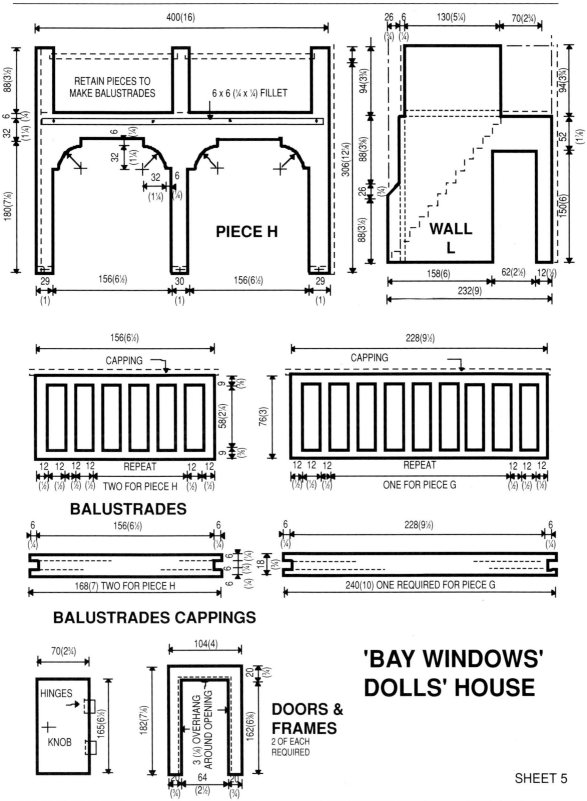

PIECE H

400(16)
88(3½)
6
32 (1¼)
180(7⅛)
RETAIN PIECES TO MAKE BALUSTRADES
6 x 6 (¼ x ¼) FILLET
6 (¼)
32 (1¼)
32 (1¼)
6 (¼)
306(12⅛)
29 (1)
156(6½)
30 (1)
156(6½)
29 (1)

WALL L

26 (¾)
6 (¼)
130(5¼)
70(2¾)
94(3¾)
94(3¾)
88(3⅜)
52 (1⅞)
26 (¾)
88(3½)
150(6)
158(6)
62(2½)
12(½)
232(9)

BALUSTRADES

156(6½)
CAPPING
9 (⅜)
58(2¼)
9 (⅜)
12 12 12 12 REPEAT 12 12
(½) (½) (½) (½) (½) (½)
TWO FOR PIECE H

228(9½)
CAPPING
76(3)
12 12 12 REPEAT 12 12 12
(½) (½) (½) (½) (½) (½)
ONE FOR PIECE G

BALUSTRADES CAPPINGS

6 (¼)
156(6½)
6 (¼)
6 (¼)
6 (¼)
18 (¾)
168(7) TWO FOR PIECE H

6 (¼)
228(9½)
6 (¼)
240(10) ONE REQUIRED FOR PIECE G

DOORS & FRAMES
2 OF EACH REQUIRED

70(2¾)
HINGES
KNOB
165(6½)

104(4)
20 (¾)
182(7⅛)
3 (⅛) OVERHANG AROUND OPENING
162(6⅜)
20 (¾)
64 (2½)
20 (¾)

'BAY WINDOWS' DOLLS' HOUSE

SHEET 5

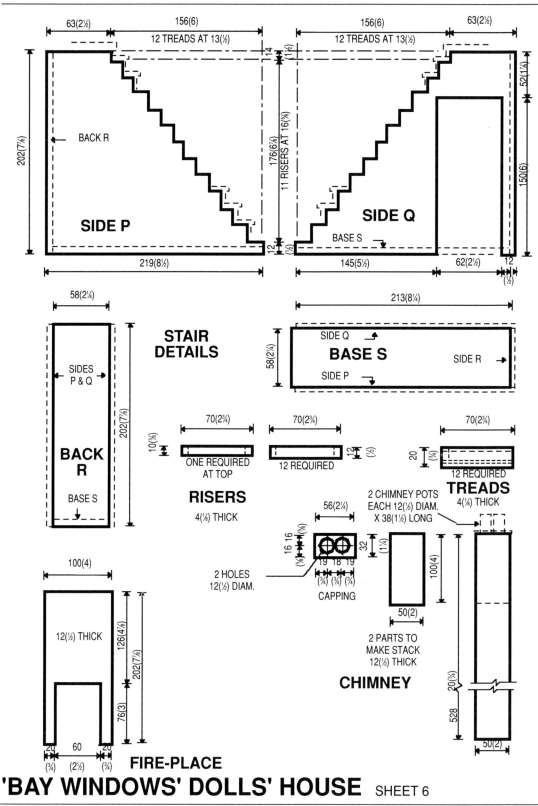

STAIR DETAILS

RISERS

TREADS

FIRE-PLACE

CHIMNEY

CAPPING

'BAY WINDOWS' DOLLS' HOUSE SHEET 6

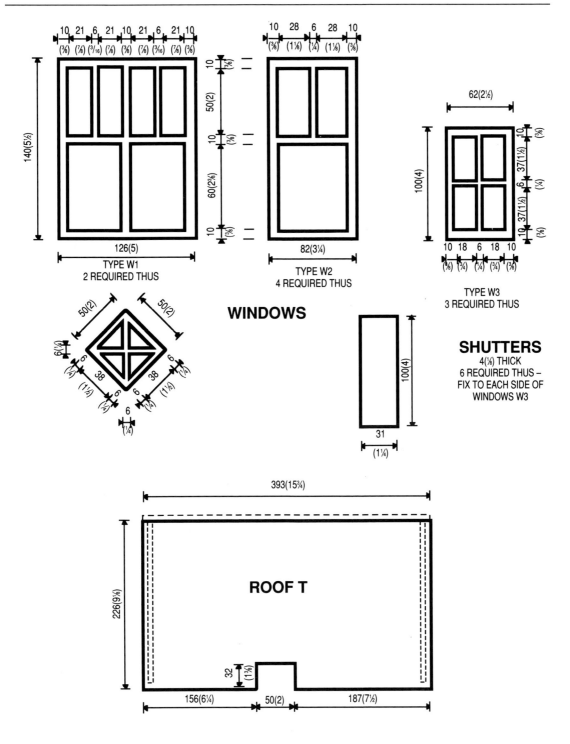

WINDOWS

TYPE W1
2 REQUIRED THUS

TYPE W2
4 REQUIRED THUS

TYPE W3
3 REQUIRED THUS

SHUTTERS
4(⅛) THICK
6 REQUIRED THUS –
FIX TO EACH SIDE OF
WINDOWS W3

ROOF T

'BAY WINDOWS' DOLLS' HOUSE SHEET 7

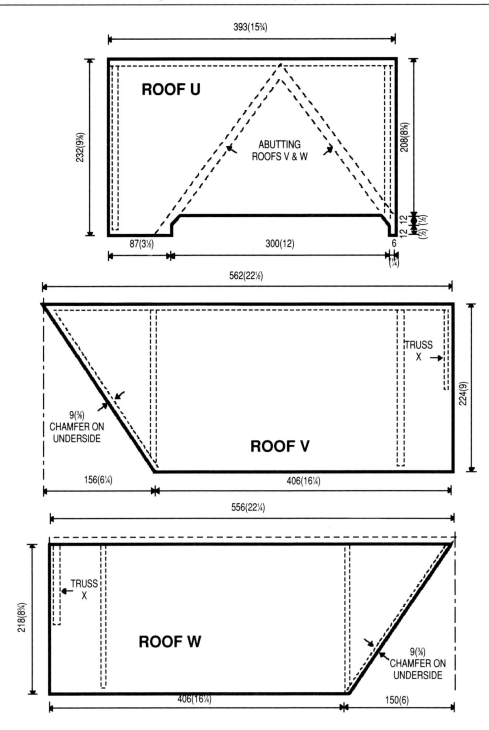

'BAY WINDOWS' DOLLS' HOUSE

SHEET 8

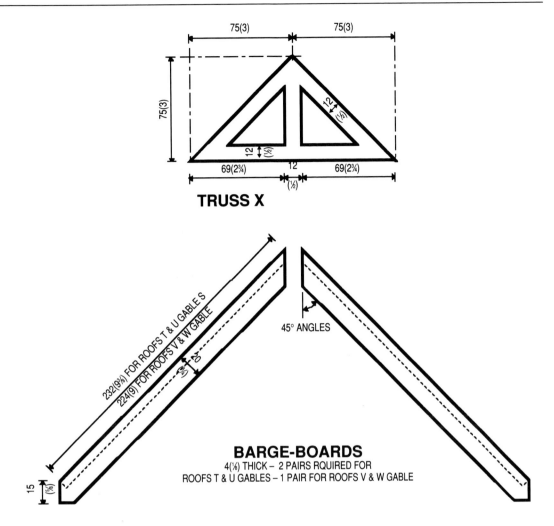

TRUSS X

BARGE-BOARDS
4(⅛) THICK – 2 PAIRS RQUIRED FOR
ROOFS T & U GABLES – 1 PAIR FOR ROOFS V & W GABLE

45° ANGLES

232(9⅜) FOR ROOFS T & U GABLES
224(9) FOR ROOFS V & W GABLE

'BAY WINDOWS' DOLLS' HOUSE

SHEET 9

PROJECT 8

GEORGIAN DOLLS' HOUSE

T his house has been designed to represent a typical Georgian town house in its style and proportions. Its scale is 1:12 (1 inch to 1 foot).

Access is by way of the back wall which is hinged in two leaves and also by way of a hinged roof giving access to an attic.

A fireplace is provided in one of the rooms, but if desired, a similar feature can be added to the other rooms. If so, it must be fixed to the room walls (s) before the house is finally assembled in a similar manner to that described for the fireplace feature in the Construction Notes.

Other features of this house are the cornices and door architrave using timber mouldings. The profile and size of the mouldings used need not necessarily be the same as those detailed on the plans but if the sizes differ, then appropriate amendments must be made to the lengths of the components made from the mouldings. However, the 6×6 mm ($\frac{1}{4}$ in $\times \frac{1}{4}$ in) rebate in the picture frame moulding is required to fit as an overlap to the 6 mm ($\frac{1}{4}$ in) thick door surround.

CUTTING LIST

$662 \times 288 \times 12$ mm ($26\frac{1}{2} \times 11\frac{1}{2} \times \frac{1}{2}$ in)   plywood

$2000 \times 1200 \times 6$ mm ($80 \times 48 \times \frac{1}{4}$ in)   plywood

$500 \times 250 \times 4$ mm ($20 \times 10 \times \frac{1}{8}$ in)   plywood

$164 \times 70 \times 1.5$ mm ($6\frac{1}{2} \times 2\frac{3}{4} \times \frac{1}{16}$ in)   plywood or card

$122 \times 15 \times 15$ mm ($4\frac{3}{4} \times \frac{5}{8} \times \frac{5}{8}$ in)   timber

$90 \times 76 \times 12$ mm ($3\frac{1}{2} \times 3 \times \frac{1}{2}$ in)   timber

$200 \times 38 \times 18$ mm ($7\frac{1}{2} \times 1\frac{1}{2} \times \frac{3}{4}$ in)   timber

$950 \times 9 \times 9$ mm ($38 \times \frac{3}{8} \times \frac{3}{8}$ in)   timber

9 mm ($\frac{3}{8}$ in) diameter $\times 100$ mm (4 in)   timber dowel

4 mm ($\frac{1}{8}$ in) diameter $\times 304$ mm (12 in)   timber dowel

$15 \times 15 \times 1535$ mm ($\frac{5}{8} \times \frac{5}{8} \times 62$ in)   cavetto moulding

$20 \times 12 \times 610$ mm ($\frac{3}{4} \times \frac{1}{2} \times 24$ in)   picture frame moulding

$12 \times 6 \times 3400$ mm ($\frac{1}{2} \times \frac{1}{4} \times 140$ in)   timber fillet

$6 \times 6 \times 1110$ mm ($\frac{1}{4} \times \frac{1}{4} \times 45$ in)   timber fillet

ANCILLARIES

$3\frac{1}{2}$ pairs 25 mm (1 in) brass hinges

3 small knobs

1 brass hook fastener

CONSTRUCTION DETAILS

1. Mark and cut out the components for the base; the floors (first and attic); walls A, B, C, D, E, F and G; and piece H.

2. Complete the cutting of the windows, door and fanlight, using the pieces cut from walls A, D and E to form these (*as described in Section 2*). Stain or paint the windows and fanlight and put them aside to dry.

3. Complete the door by cutting out the panel overlay from 1.5 mm ($\frac{1}{16}$ in) thick plywood or

card and glue this to the face of the door leaving a 3 mm ($\frac{1}{8}$ in) margin at each side. Fix one pair of 25mm (1 in) hinges to the back of the door. Fix a small knob to the door front (*detail in Project 1 plans*). Paint the door and put it aside to dry.

4. Fix the 12×6 mm ($\frac{1}{2} \times \frac{1}{4}$ in) fillets to the one edge of walls B and C (these are to provide adequate screw-fixing for the hinges for walls D and E).

5. Fix the 6×6 mm ($\frac{1}{4} \times \frac{1}{4}$ in) floor support fillets to walls B and C.

6. Cut out the parts forming the fireplace and fix these to wall B commencing with the 12 mm ($\frac{1}{2}$ in) thick piece which is glued and pinned through the wall into it – ensure that it is located with a 12 mm ($\frac{1}{2}$ in) clearance from the bottom of the wall to clear the base. Next glue and pin the mantle shelf and then the middle shelf – also pinning through the wall into their back edges.

If it is decided to provide other rooms with a similar feature now is the time to fix these to walls B and/or C before proceeding further.

7. Cut from 4 mm ($\frac{1}{8}$ in) thick plywood the window linings (*as described in Section 2*) and glue and pin these around the sides and tops of the window openings in walls A, D and E, ensuring that they overlap the opening edges by 3 mm ($\frac{1}{8}$ in). If desired, the four windows in the back walls D and E can be finished with plain linings made from 12×4 mm ($\frac{1}{2} \times \frac{1}{8}$ in) strips instead of the simulated masonry linings. These strips also should be fixed to overlap the opening edges by 3 mm ($\frac{1}{8}$ in) as for the other window linings.

8. Cut from 9×9 mm ($\frac{3}{8} \times \frac{3}{8}$ in) timber the window sills and fix these to the bottoms of the window openings in walls A, D and E to complete the window lining surrounds.

9. Cut out the door surround and fix it to the front of wall A so that it forms an overlap of 3 mm ($\frac{1}{8}$ in) to the door opening edges. (Note that the bottom of this surround is to be flush with the bottom of wall A.)

10. Cut from the picture frame moulding the parts to make the door architrave and glue and pin these around the door surround with the rebate in the moulding overlapping the surround and the mitred ends neatly fitting. (Note that it will be necessary to amend the dimensions as given on the plans if a different size of moulding is used.)

11. Construct the door cornice by firstly fixing the 15 × 15 × 122 mm ($\frac{5}{8} \times \frac{5}{8} \times 4\frac{3}{4}$ in) timber block to wall A immediately above the door architrave and centred on the door opening. Then cut from the 15 × 15 mm ($\frac{5}{8} \times \frac{5}{8}$ in) cavetto moulding the pieces to form the cornice and glue and pin these to the front and ends of the block with their mitred ends neatly joined.

12. Glue the windows and fanlight into the openings in walls A, D and E from which they were originally cut.

13. Fix the door into its opening in wall A by securing the hinges so that it opens inwards with the door stops formed by the overlap of the surround previously fixed (*item* 9).

14. Cut out the components for the stair and construct it in accordance with the instructions given in Section 2 and as follows:

i. Glue and pin piece W to the stair base and pieces X and Y to the base and to piece W.

ii. Glue the treads and risers to pieces X and Y commencing with the bottom riser, then the bottom tread, the next riser, the next tread, *et seq* to completion.

iii. Glue and pin piece Z to the side of stair piece Y with the profiles of the cut-outs to

clear the door (when open) coinciding on each piece.

iv. Glue and pin piece V to piece Z so that it will overhang the stair.

15. Glue and pin the completed stair assembly to wall G with its base flush with the bottom of wall G. Pin through G into the end of piece V (ensure that there is a 38 mm ($1\frac{1}{2}$ in) clearance left between the face of piece V and the edge of the door opening in wall G to accommodate the attic ladder).

16. Cut out the pieces required to make the attic ladder and construct it as described in Section 2. After completion and time allowed for the glued rungs to set hard, fix the ladder to wall G in the space between the face of piece V and the side of the door opening.

17. This is a convenient time to apply the desired finish (paint, varnish, wallpaper, or combinations of these) to the inside faces of the walls, to the stair and to the tops and undersides of the base and the first floor, ensuring that the applied finish is kept clear of the positions where walls/floors are fixed to each other. Allow to dry.

18. Glue and screw the front wall A to the base using 4 No $\frac{5}{8}$ in × 4 countersunk (c/s) screws.

19. Glue and screw the side wall B to the base using 2 No $\frac{5}{8}$ in × 4 c/s screws and pin through B into the end of wall A.

20. Glue and slide wall G (with the stair assembly) into the first floor, as described in Section 2 (interlocking joint).

21. Glue and slide wall F into the first floor.

22. Glue and insert the assembly of the first floor with walls F and G and the stair onto the base with one edge of the floor seated on the fillet fixed to wall B.

23. Immediately following the action of instruction 22, glue and screw the side wall C to the base using 2 No $\frac{5}{8}$ in × 4 c/s screws and ensuring that the edge of the first floor is seated on the fillet fixed to C. Pin through C into the end of wall A. Complete the assembly so far by pinning through walls A, B and C into the edges and ends of the first floor and walls F and G, and screw from below and through the base into the base of the stair using a $\frac{3}{4}$ in × 6 c/s screw.

24. Cut out the trap door from the attic floor and refix it in its opening with a 25 mm (1 in) hinge.

25. Cut out the two gables J and the two pieces K. Glue and pin the ends of pieces K into the notches formed in gables J. Ensure that the assembly is square and put it aside to allow the glued joints to set firm.

26. Glue and pin the assembly of gables J and pieces K to the top of the attic floor (located in accordance with the dimensions given on the attic floor plan).

27. Glue and insert the attic floor (with the assembly of gables J and pieces K) so that it is seated on the fillets fixed to walls B and C and on the tops of walls F and G. Pin through walls A, B and C into the edges of the attic floor, and through the floor into the tops of walls F and G.

28. Glue and pin piece H to the back edge of the attic floor and the top ends of walls B and C.

29. Cut from the 15 × 15 mm ($\frac{5}{8}$ × $\frac{5}{8}$ in) cavetto moulding pieces to fit and form the main cornice around the top of the front (wall A) and sides (walls B and C). The two ends of the front piece and one end of each of the side pieces are to be mitred 45°. Glue and pin these pieces into their positions with the mitres neatly joined where they meet and return at the corners.

30. Cut out the two quoins from 4 mm ($\frac{1}{8}$ in) thick plywood and glue and pin one to each end of the front walls A. The grooves to simulate masonry joints should be cut as described in Project 10, the Corner Shop.

31. Cut lengths from 28 × 6 mm ($\frac{7}{8}$ × $\frac{1}{4}$ in) plywood to fit and form a plinth around the base at the front and sides and glue and pin these into position.

32. Cut out the pieces for roofs L and M, the two dormer windows, and the two sets of

33. After cutting the chamfers on the dormer cheeks glue and pin these to the backs of the windows (*refer to Section 2 for dormer window construction*).

34. Glue and pin the 12 × 6 mm ($\frac{1}{2}$ × $\frac{1}{4}$ in) length of fillet to the underside of roof M ensuring that a 6 mm ($\frac{1}{4}$ in) space is left at each end to allow this roof to seat on gables J.

35. Cut out the parts forming the two chimneys (stacks, cappings and pots). Do not assemble at this stage.

36. Secure the two chimney stacks to the top of roof M by glueing and screwing into them from below and through the roof using a $\frac{5}{8}$ in × 4 c/s screw for each.

37. With roof M loosely-fitted in its required position on gables J, check for the fit of the two dormer windows/cheeks assemblies. The bottoms of the windows should pass through the wider part of the apertures formed in the roof and locate behind piece K which is fixed to the attic floor. The cheeks should seat firmly on the roof. Make any adjustments as necessary to ensure a good fit and when satisfied, glue and pin through the roof into the cheeks to secure the windows.

38. Glue and pin the completed assembly of roof M with the dormer windows and chimney stacks onto the gables J. (Note that the top edge of this roof is to be 6 mm ($\frac{1}{4}$ in) below the apex (top) of the gable to allow clearance for the 6 mm ($\frac{1}{4}$ in) thickness of the fillet to be fixed to the hinged roof L.)

39. Cut the chamfers on the edges of the two sets of dormer roofs and check them for a proper fit before glueing and pinning them into position on the windows and roof.

40. Complete the two chimneys by glueing and pinning the cappings onto the tops of the stacks (fixed to the roof) and glue and insert the pots into the holes cut in the cappings to receive them.

41. Glue and pin the 12 × 6 mm ($\frac{1}{2}$ × $\frac{1}{4}$ in) length of fillet (with a 6 × 6 mm ($\frac{1}{4}$ × $\frac{1}{4}$ in) cut–out at each end) to the underside of roof L. Recess the under–face of the fillet to receive the two 25 mm (1 in) hinges and fix these into position. Fix the small knob to the top surface of of L.

42. With roof L seated in its required position on the gables J, mark the location of the two

hinges on the top edge of roof M and cut recesses at these positions to receive the hinges, which can then be screwed into position to secure roof L as a hinged access 'lid'.

43. Glue and pin the 12 × 6 mm ($\frac{1}{2}$ × $\frac{1}{4}$ in) fillets to the outside faces of the two ends of wall E and the one end of wall D (the fillet at the 'meeting' edge of wall E is to project 3 mm ($\frac{1}{8}$ in) to act as a stop to the 'meeting' edge of wall D). Secure one pair of 25 mm (1 in) hinges to the inside face of the outer edge of each wall. Fix a small knob to the outside face of each wall.

44. With walls D and E placed in their required positions at the back of the house, mark the location of the two pairs of hinges on the edges of walls B and C and cut recesses at these positions to receive the hinges which can then be screwed into their positions to secure walls D and E as access 'doors'. Fix the small hook fastener to the top of wall E so that it can engage into a small dome-headed screw ($\frac{3}{8}$ in × 2) fixed into piece H. This will secure walls D and E in the closed position.

45. Complete the house by applying the desired finish of paint or varnish.

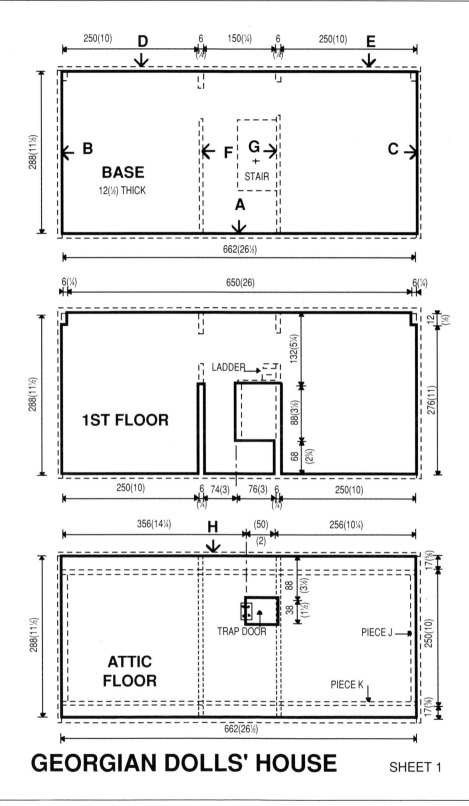

250(10)   D   6 (¼)   150(¼)   6 (¼)   250(10)   E

288(11½)

B   F   G   C
BASE   STAIR
12(½) THICK
A

662(26½)

6(¼)   650(26)   6(¼)

12 (½)

288(11½)   132(5¼)   276(11)

LADDER

88(3½)

1ST FLOOR

68 (2¾)

250(10)   6 (¼)   74(3)   76(3)   6 (¼)   250(10)

356(14¼)   H   (50) (2)   256(10¼)

17(⅝)

288(11½)   88 (3½)   250(10)

38 (1½)

TRAP DOOR   PIECE J

ATTIC
FLOOR

PIECE K

17(⅝)

662(26½)

GEORGIAN DOLLS' HOUSE   SHEET 1

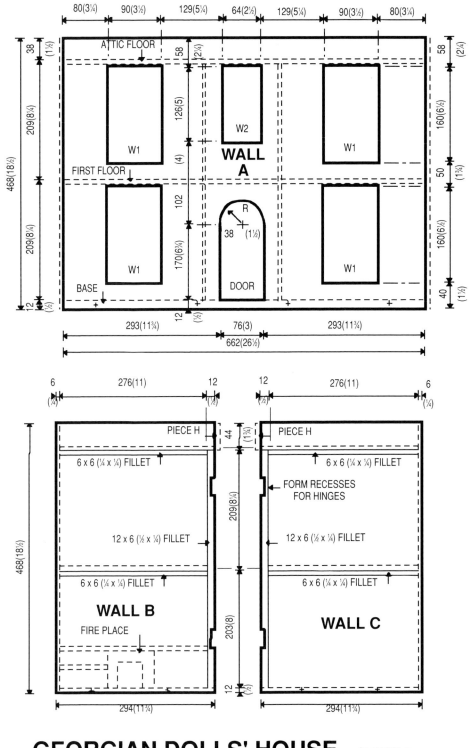

GEORGIAN DOLLS' HOUSE   SHEET 2

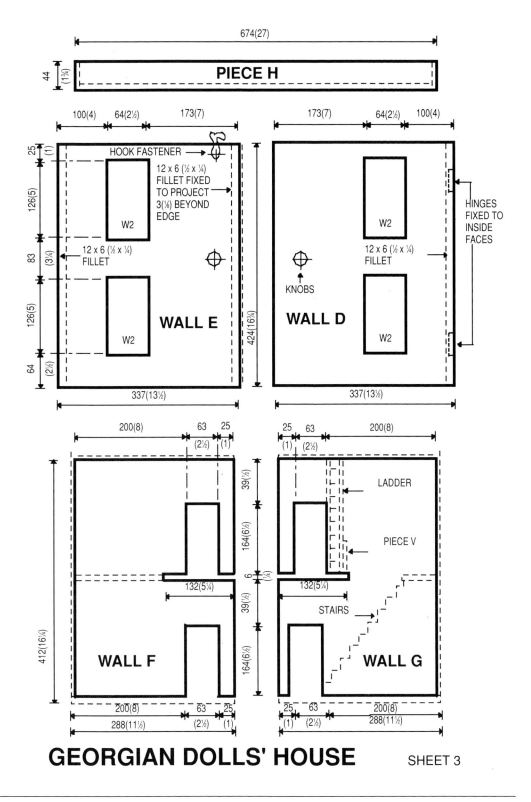

674(27)

44 (1¾)

PIECE H

100(4) 64(2½) 173(7) 173(7) 88(2½) 100(4)

25 (1)

HOOK FASTENER

12 x 6 (½ x ¼) FILLET FIXED TO PROJECT 3(⅛) BEYOND EDGE

126(5)

W2

12 x 6 (½ x ¼) FILLET

83 (3¼)

126(5)

W2

WALL E

64 (2½)

337(13½)

HINGES FIXED TO INSIDE FACES

W2

12 x 6 (½ x ¼) FILLET

KNOBS

WALL D

W2

424(16¾)

337(13½)

200(8) 63 (2½) 25 (1) 25 (1) 63 (2½) 200(8)

39 (1½)

LADDER

164(6½)

PIECE V

132(5¼)

6 (¼)

132(5¼)

39 (1½)

STAIRS

412(16¼)

164(6½)

WALL F

WALL G

200(8) 63 (2½) 25 (1) 25 (1) 63 (2½) 200(8)

288(11½)

288(11½)

GEORGIAN DOLLS' HOUSE   SHEET 3

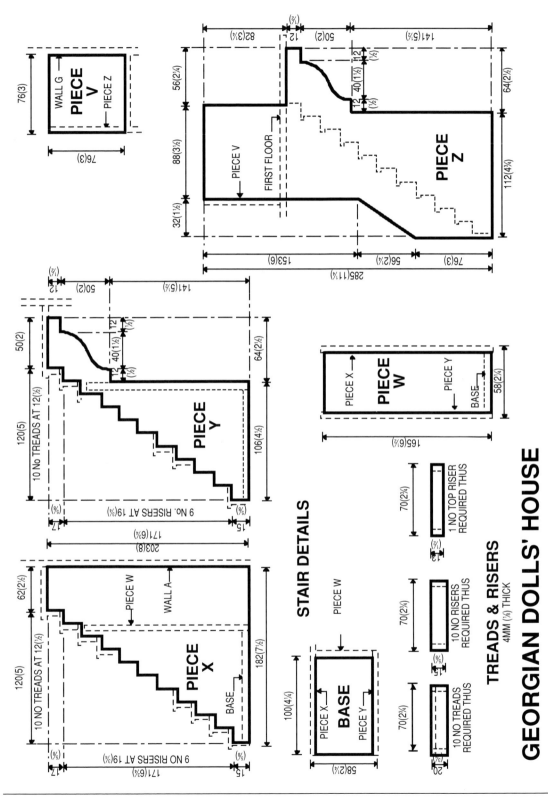

STAIR DETAILS

GEORGIAN DOLLS' HOUSE

TREADS & RISERS
4MM (⅛) THICK

SHEET 4

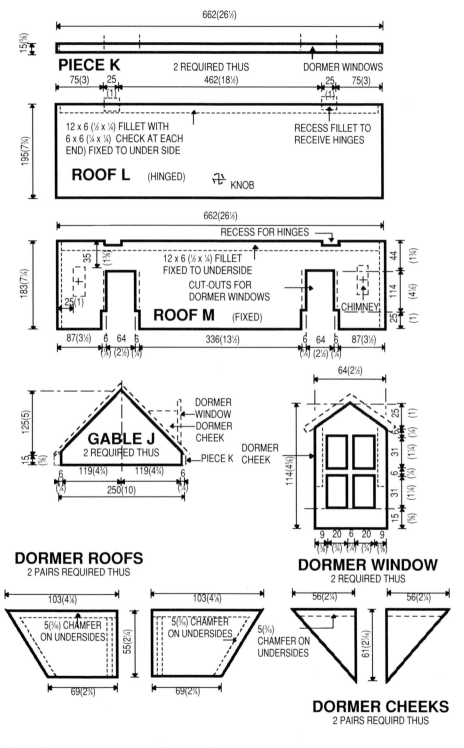

662(26½)

15(⅝)

PIECE K   2 REQUIRED THUS   DORMER WINDOWS

75(3)   25   462(18½)   25   75(3)
(1)   (1)

195(7¾)

12 x 6 (½ x ¼) FILLET WITH
6 x 6 (¼ x ¼) CHECK AT EACH
END) FIXED TO UNDER SIDE

RECESS FILLET TO
RECEIVE HINGES

ROOF L   (HINGED)   KNOB

662(26½)

RECESS FOR HINGES

183(7¼)

35 (1⅜)

12 x 6 (½ x ¼) FILLET
FIXED TO UNDERSIDE

CUT-OUTS FOR
DORMER WINDOWS

44 (1¾)

114 (4½)

25(1)

25 (1)

ROOF M   (FIXED)

CHIMNEY

87(3½)   6   64   6   336(13½)   6   64   6   87(3½)
(¼) (2½) (¼)   (¼) (2½) (¼)

125(5)

GABLE J
2 REQUIRED THUS

DORMER
WINDOW
DORMER
CHEEK

PIECE K   DORMER
CHEEK

15 (⅝)

6 (¼)   119(4¾)   119(4¾)   6 (¼)
250(10)

64(2½)

25 (1)
6 (¼)

114(4⅝)

31 (1¼)

6 (¼)

31 (1¼)

15 (⅝)

9   20   6   20   9
(⅜) (¾) (¼) (¾) (⅜)

DORMER WINDOW
2 REQUIRED THUS

DORMER ROOFS
2 PAIRS REQUIRED THUS

103(4⅛)

5(³/₁₆) CHAMFER
ON UNDERSIDES

55(2¼)

69(2¾)

103(4⅛)

5(³/₁₆) CHAMFER
ON UNDERSIDES

69(2¾)

56(2¼)

5(³/₁₆)
CHAMFER ON
UNDERSIDES

56(2¼)

61(2⅞)

DORMER CHEEKS
2 PAIRS REQUIRD THUS

GEORGIAN DOLLS' HOUSE   SHEET 5

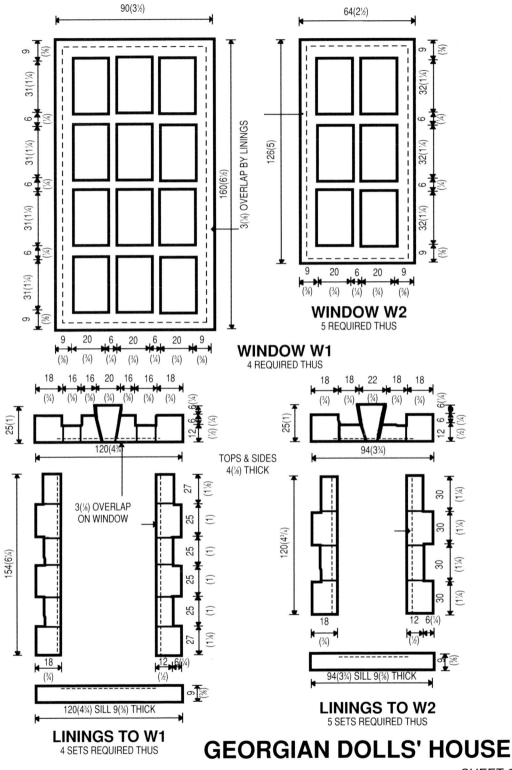

90(3½)

9 (⅜)
31(1¼)
6 (¼)
31(1¼)
6 (¼)
31(1¼)
6 (¼)
31(1¼)
9 (⅜)

160(6½)

3(⅛) OVERLAP BY LININGS

9 (⅜) 20 (¾) 6 (¼) 20 (¾) 6 (¼) 20 (¾) 9 (⅜)

WINDOW W1
4 REQUIRED THUS

64(2½)

9 (⅜)
32(1¼)
6 (¼)
32(1¼)
6 (¼)
32(1¼)
9 (⅜)

126(5)

9 (⅜) 20 (¾) 6 (¼) 20 (¾) 9 (⅜)

WINDOW W2
5 REQUIRED THUS

18 (¾) 16 (⅝) 16 (⅝) 20 (¾) 16 (⅝) 16 (⅝) 18 (¾)

25(1)

12 6 (½)(¼) 6(¼)

120(4¾)

3(⅛) OVERLAP ON WINDOW

TOPS & SIDES
4(⅛) THICK

18 (¾) 18 (¾) 22 (¾) 18 (¾) 18 (¾)

25(1)

12 6 (½)(¼) 6(¼)

94(3¾)

27 (1⅛)
25 (1)
25 (1)
25 (1)
25 (1)
27 (1⅛)

154(6¼)

30 (1¼)
30 (1¼)
30 (1¼)
30 (1¼)

120(4¾)

18 (¾)

12 6(¼) (½)

18 (¾) 12 6(¼) (½)

9 (⅜)

120(4¾) SILL 9(⅜) THICK

LININGS TO W1
4 SETS REQUIRED THUS

9 (⅜)

94(3¾) SILL 9(⅜) THICK

LININGS TO W2
5 SETS REQUIRED THUS

GEORGIAN DOLLS' HOUSE
SHEET 6

FANLIGHT

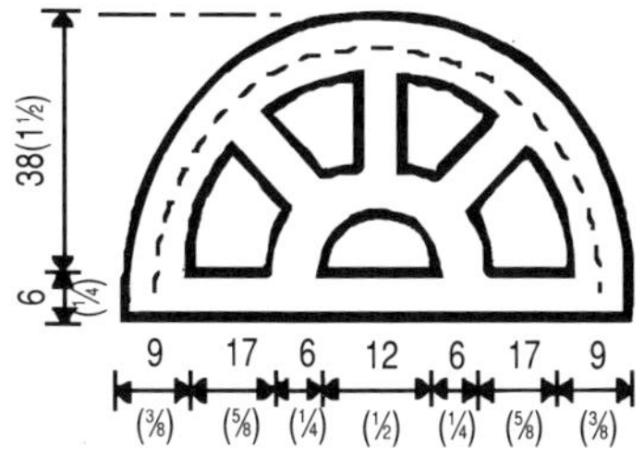

38(1½)
6
(¼)
9 17 6 12 6 17 9
(⅜) (⅝) (¼) (½) (¼) (⅝) (⅜)

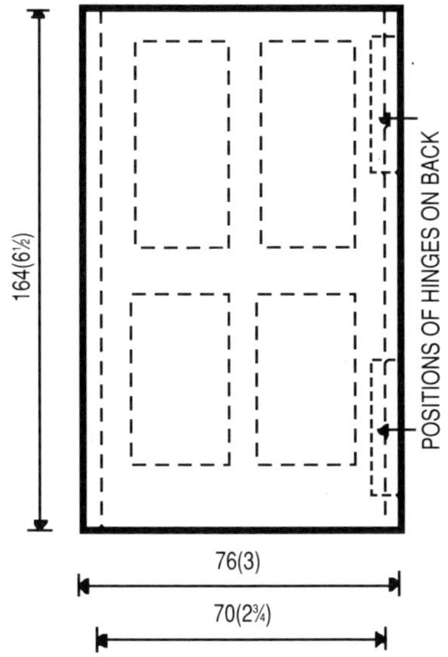

164(6½)
POSITIONS OF HINGES ON BACK
76(3)
70(2¾)

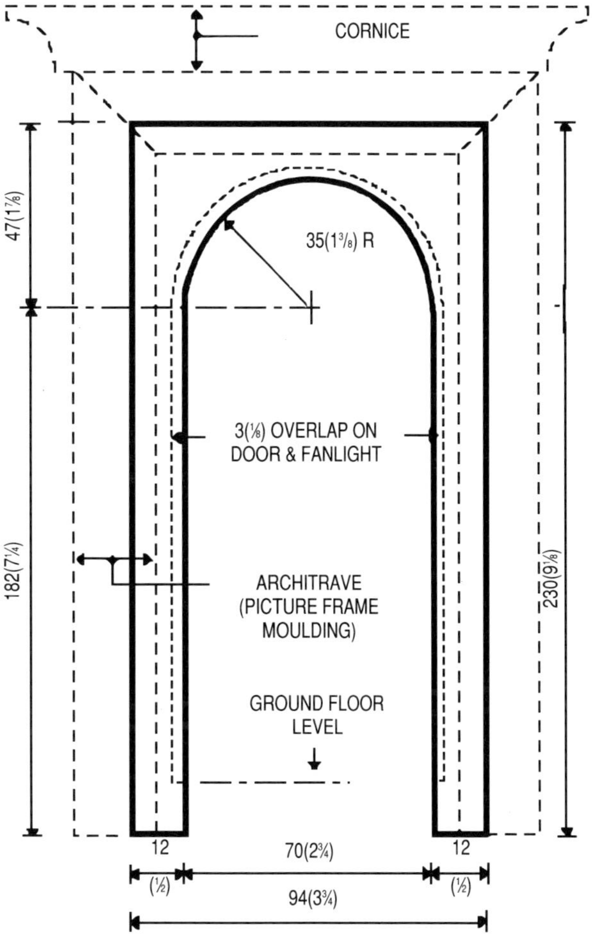

CORNICE
47(1⅞)
35(1⅜) R
3(⅛) OVERLAP ON
DOOR & FANLIGHT
182(7¼)
ARCHITRAVE
(PICTURE FRAME
MOULDING)
GROUND FLOOR
LEVEL
230(9⅛)
12
70(2¾)
12
(½)
(½)
94(3¾)

DOOR SURROUND

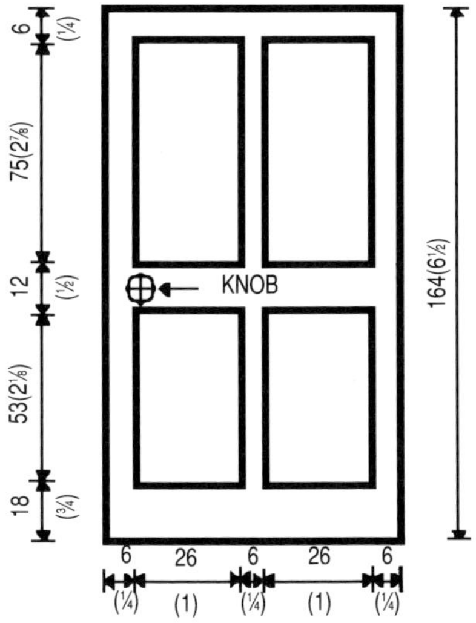

6
(¼)
75(2⅞)
12
(½)
KNOB
53(2⅛)
18
(¾)
164(6½)
6 26 6 26 6
(¼) (1) (¼) (1) (¼)

PANEL OVERLAY

1.5 (¼) THICK PLYWOOD OR CARD

GEORGIAN DOLLS' HOUSE

SHEET 7

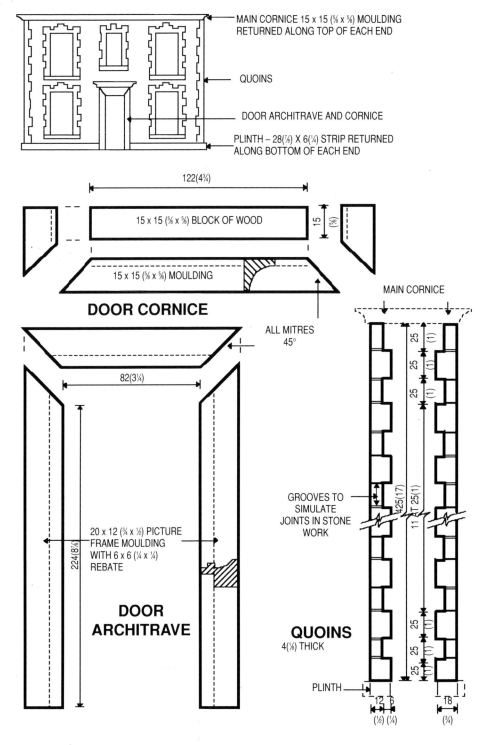

MAIN CORNICE 15 x 15 (⅝ x ⅝) MOULDING
RETURNED ALONG TOP OF EACH END

QUOINS

DOOR ARCHITRAVE AND CORNICE

PLINTH – 28(⅞) X 6(¼) STRIP RETURNED
ALONG BOTTOM OF EACH END

122(4¾)

15 x 15 (⅝ x ⅝) BLOCK OF WOOD

15
(⅝)

15 x 15 (⅝ x ⅝) MOULDING

DOOR CORNICE

ALL MITRES
45°

82(3¼)

20 x 12 (¾ x ½) PICTURE
FRAME MOULDING
WITH 6 x 6 (¼ x ¼)
REBATE

224(8⅞)

**DOOR
ARCHITRAVE**

MAIN CORNICE

25 (1)
25 (1)
25 (1)

GROOVES TO
SIMULATE
JOINTS IN STONE
WORK

425(17)
11 AT 25(1)

25 (1)
25 (1)
25 (1)

QUOINS
4(⅛) THICK

PLINTH

12 6
(½) (¼)

18
(¾)

GEORGIAN DOLLS' HOUSE   SHEET 8

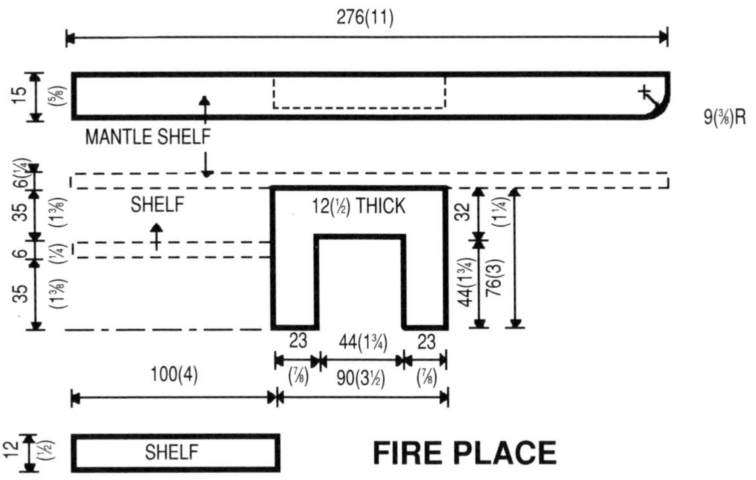
276(11)
15 (⅝)
MANTLE SHELF
9(⅜)R
6(¼)
35 (1⅜)
6 (¼)
35 (1⅜)
SHELF
12(½) THICK
32 (1¼)
44(1¾)
76(3)
23 (⅞)
44(1¾)
23 (⅞)
90(3½)
100(4)
12 (½)
SHELF

FIRE PLACE

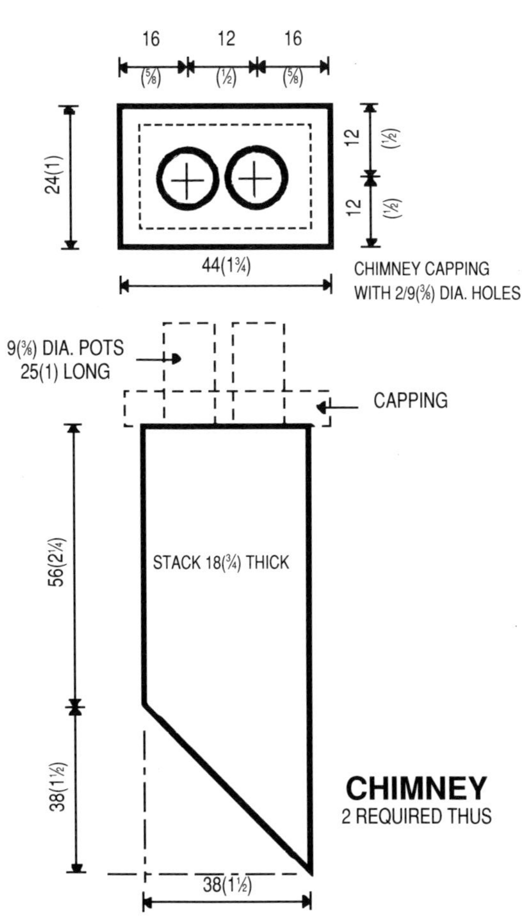
16 (⅝)
12 (½)
16 (⅝)
24(1)
12 (½)
12 (½)
44(1¾)
CHIMNEY CAPPING
WITH 2/9(⅜) DIA. HOLES
9(⅜) DIA. POTS
25(1) LONG
CAPPING
STACK 18(¾) THICK
56(2¼)
38(1½)
38(1½)

CHIMNEY
2 REQUIRED THUS

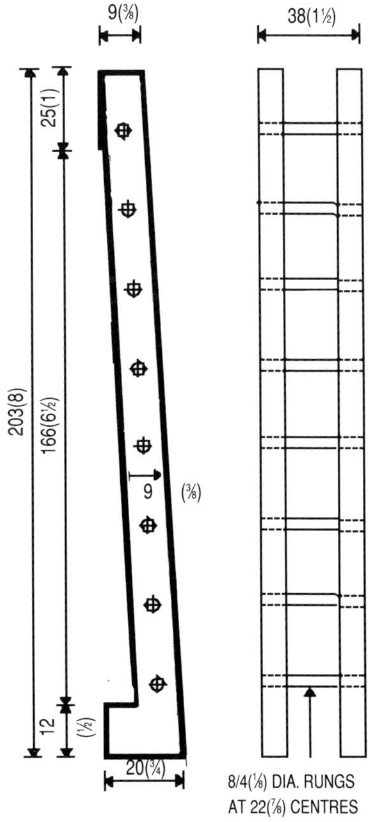
9(⅜)
38(1½)
203(8)
25(1)
166(6½)
9 (⅜)
12 (½)
20(¾)
8/4(⅛) DIA. RUNGS
AT 22(⅞) CENTRES

ATTIC LADDER

GEORGIAN DOLLS' HOUSE

PROJECT 9

A FARM

This attractive toy comprises a farmhouse, a pigsty, a cow-shed with stables and a cart-shed with hay-bay. The four parts can be left as separate units which a child can arrange at will, or they can be secured to a base-board to produce a layout with an overall size of 500 × 500 mm (20 × 20 in). A distinctive feature is the clock-tower located on the cart-shed/hay-bay roof

Except for the farmhouse, sufficient doorway openings of a suitable size have been provided in the buildings to allow adequate access to their interiors by small hands.

The toy is of proportions suitable to be used with the toy farmyard animals and implements which are obtainable at a majority of toy shops and it is approximately 1/32 ($\frac{3}{8}$ inch to a foot) scale. The toy portrayed in the photograph has been finished with a flint-stone patterned paper on the walls, slate patterned paper on the pitched roofs, and varnish elsewhere.

The 'Construction Details' describe the process of making each of the four units separately.

CUTTING LIST

500 × 500 × 4 mm (20 × 20 × $\frac{1}{8}$ in)	plywood or hardboard (optional)
1000 × 680 × 6 mm (40 × 27 × $\frac{1}{4}$ in)	plywood
750 × 350 × 4 mm (30 × 14 × $\frac{1}{8}$ in)	plywood
38 × 32 × 19 mm (1$\frac{1}{2}$ × 1$\frac{1}{4}$ × $\frac{3}{4}$ in)	timber
38 × 26 × 26 mm (1$\frac{1}{2}$ × 1 × 1 in)	timber
38 × 38 × 38 mm (1$\frac{1}{2}$ × 1$\frac{1}{2}$ × 1$\frac{1}{2}$)	timber

CONSTRUCTION DETAILS

Farmhouse

1. Mark and cut out the components to form the base, walls A, B, C and D, and the porch components E, F (2 pieces) and G.

2. Complete the cutting of the 8 windows using the pieces previously cut from walls A and B to form their openings (*as described in Section 2*). Paint or varnish the completed windows before fixing them.

The windows can be glued back into the openings from which they were originally cut at this stage, or they can be fixed at a later stage of assembly after the required finish has been applied to the walls.

3. Glue and pin the triangular-shaped piece G to the outside face of wall A so that it is centred over the door opening with its bottom edge flush with the top of the door opening. This piece will provide support for the porch roof.

4. Glue and pin wall A to the base. Note that the notches cut out from each side of the bottom

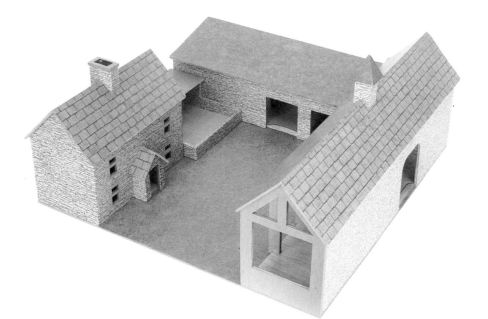

of the door opening should neatly fit over the porch projection on the base.

5. Glue and pin wall B to the base.

6. Glue and pin gable wall C to the base and to the ends of walls A and B.

7. Glue and pin gable wall D to the base and to the ends of walls A and B.

8. Glue and pin the two porch walls F to the base porch projection and pin through wall A into the edges of walls F.

9. Glue and pin porch wall E to the base porch projection and to the edges of walls F.

This is an opportune time to paint or varnish the inside of this unit and to apply the required finish to the outside of the walls, after which the windows can be glued back into their openings if this was not done with instruction 2.

10. Cut out the four pieces to form the main and porch roofs (4 mm ($\frac{1}{8}$ in) thick) as well as the two parts to make the chimney.

11. Glue and screw the chimney stack to roof H using a $\frac{1}{2}$ in × 4 countersunk (c/s) screw.

12. Glue and pin roof J onto the top edges of one side of gable walls C and D.

13. Apply glue along the top edge of roof J and glue and pin roof H (with the chimney stack) onto the top edges of the other side of gable walls C and D. The roof H ridge should seat firmly against the glued contact edge of roof J, and pressure should be maintained along this edge until the glue has achieved a firm bond.

14. Complete the chimney by glueing and pinning the capping piece to the top of the stack previously fixed to the roof.

15. Glue and pin porch roof L to the top edges of one side of wall E and piece G (fixed to wall A).

16. Apply glue to the top edge of roof L and glue and pin roof K to the other side top edges of wall E and piece G, maintaining pressure along the ridge joint as described in instruction 13.

17. Complete the farmhouse by applying the desired finish to the roofs and chimney.

Pigsty

1. Mark and cut out the base and walls A, B, C, D and E.

2. Glue and pin wall B to the base.

3. Glue and pin wall C to the base.

4. Glue and pin wall A to the base and to the ends of walls B and C.

5. Glue and pin wall D to wall B. Pin through wall B into the end edge of wall D and through the base into the bottom edge of wall D.

6. Glue and pin wall E to the base and into the ends of walls B and C.

This is an opportune time to apply the required finishes to the unit so far assembled.

7. Glue out the roof F (4 mm ($\frac{1}{8}$ in) thick and glue and pin it to the tops of walls A, B, C and D.

8. Complete the pigsty by applying the desired finish to the roof.

Cart-shed/stables

1. Mark and cut out the base, walls A, B, C, D, E and F.

2. Glue and pin wall B to the base.

3. Glue and pin wall C to the base and to the end of wall B.

4. Glue and pin wall D to the base and the end of wall B.

5. Glue and pin wall A to the base and to the ends of walls C and D.

6. Glue and fix into position wall E. Pin into its end edges through walls A and B.

7. Glue and fix into position wall F (with its high end against wall A). Pin into its end edges through walls A and B.

This is an opportune time to apply the required finishes to the unit so far assembled.

8. Cut out the roof G (4 mm ($\frac{1}{8}$ in) thick) and glue and pin it to the tops of walls C, D and E.

9. Complete the cow-shed/stable by applying the desired finish to the roof.

Cart-shed/hay-bay

1. Mark and cut out the base, walls A, B, C and D, and Frames E, F and G.

2. Glue and pin wall A to the base.

3. Glue and pin wall B to the base.

4. Glue and pin gable wall C to the base and to the ends of walls A and B.

5. Glue wall D and fix it into its position. Pin through it into the end of wall B and pin through wall A into the edge of wall D.

6. Glue and pin frame G to the base and to the end of wall A.

7. Glue frame E and fix it into its position with the front 'leg' located in the slot cut into the base to receive it. Pin through wall A into the edge of the back 'leg'.

8. Fix frame F by repeating instruction 7.

This is an opportune time to apply the required finishes to the unit so far assembled.

9. Cut out the roof H and J components as well as the two parts to make the clock-tower. It is recommended that the pyramidical shape of the tower cap be cut from the end of a piece of 38 × 38 mm ($1\frac{1}{2}$ × $1\frac{1}{2}$ ins) timber using a tenon saw, and cut from the length after completing the shaping.

10. Glue and fix the clock-tower cap to its base and maintain under pressure until the glue has achieved a firm bond. Glue and screw the completed tower to roof J using a $\frac{1}{2}$ in × 4 c/s screw.

11. Glue and pin roof H onto the top edges of one side of walls C and D, and frames E, F and G.

12. Apply glue along the top edge of roof H and glue and pin roof J (with the clock-tower) onto the top edges of the other side of walls C and D, and frames E, F and G. The roof J ridge should seat firmly against the glued contact edge of roof H, and pressure should be maintained along this joint until the glue has achieved a firm bond.

13. Complete the cart-shed/hay-bay by applying the desired finishes to the roof and clock-tower. A clock face can be cut from a thin piece of card with the hands and numbers marked on it in black ink (waterproof). This can then be glued to the tower wall.

If the units are to be fixed to a base, cut this from 4 mm ($\frac{1}{8}$ in) thick plywood or hardboard. Glue and screw each unit into its position on the base as indicated on the plans, using $\frac{1}{4}$ × 4 c/s screws (4 to each of the farm-house, pig-sty and cow-shed/stable units, and 6 to the cart-shed/hay-bay unit). If the screws should project through the surface of the unit bases in positions where they might be accessible to small fingers, they should be filed down flush with the base surfaces.

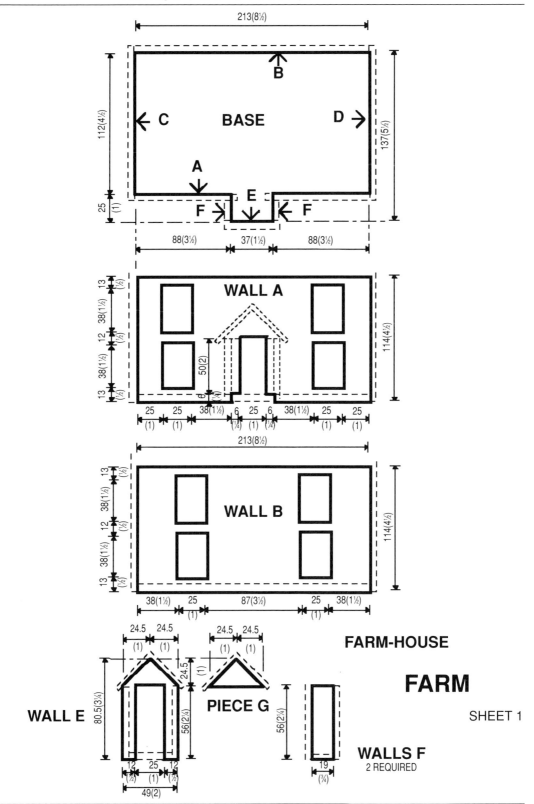

213(8½)

B

112(4½)

C   **BASE**   D

137(5½)

A

E

F   F

25(1)

88(3½)   37(1½)   88(3½)

13(½)

38(1½)

12(½)

38(1½)

13(½)

WALL A

114(4½)

50(2)

6(¼)

25(1)   25(1)   38(1½)   6(¼)   25(1)   6(¼)   38(1½)   25(1)   25(1)

213(8½)

13(½)

38(1½)

12(½)

38(1½)

13(½)

WALL B

114(4½)

38(1½)   25(1)   87(3½)   25(1)   38(1½)

24.5(1)   24.5(1)   24.5(1)   24.5(1)

FARM-HOUSE

24.5(1)

FARM

80.5(3¼)

56(2¼)

56(2¼)

WALL E

PIECE G

SHEET 1

12(½)   25(1)   12(½)

49(2)

19(¾)

WALLS F
2 REQUIRED

120

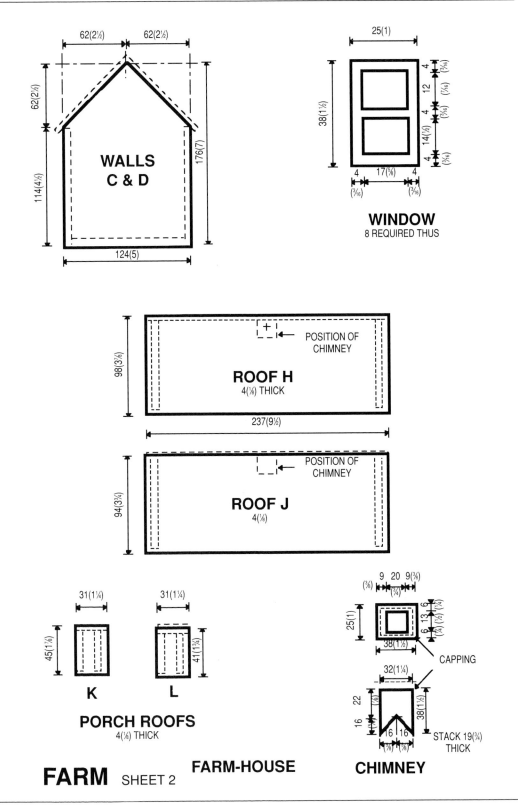

62(2½)   62(2½)

62(2½)

**WALLS
C & D**

176(7)

114(4½)

124(5)

25(1)

38(1½)

4 (³⁄₁₆)

12 (⁷⁄₁₆)

4 (³⁄₁₆)

14(½) (⁷⁄₁₆)

4 (³⁄₁₆)

4 (³⁄₁₆)   17(⅝)   4 (³⁄₁₆)

WINDOW
8 REQUIRED THUS

POSITION OF
CHIMNEY

98(3⅞)

ROOF H
4(⅛) THICK

237(9½)

POSITION OF
CHIMNEY

94(3¾)

ROOF J
4(⅛)

31(1¼)   31(1¼)

45(1⅞)   41(1¾)

K   **L**

PORCH ROOFS
4(⅛) THICK

9 20 9(⅜)
(⅜) (¾)

25(1)   6 (¼)
13 (½)
6 (¼)

38(1½)

CAPPING

32(1¼)

22 (⅞)

16 (⅝)

38(1½)

16 16
(⅝) (⅝)

STACK 19(¾)
THICK

FARM SHEET 2   **FARM-HOUSE**   **CHIMNEY**

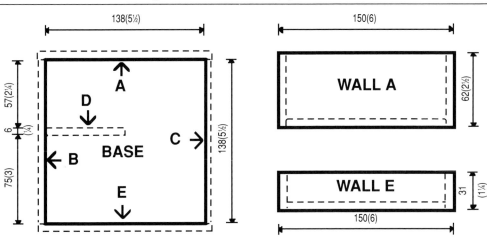

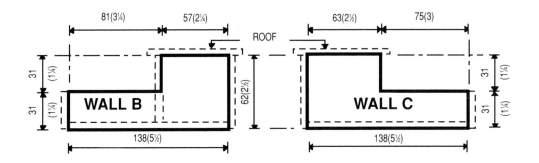

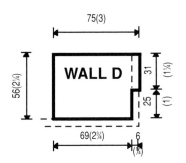

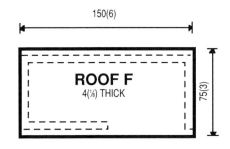

PIG-STY

FARM

SHEET 3

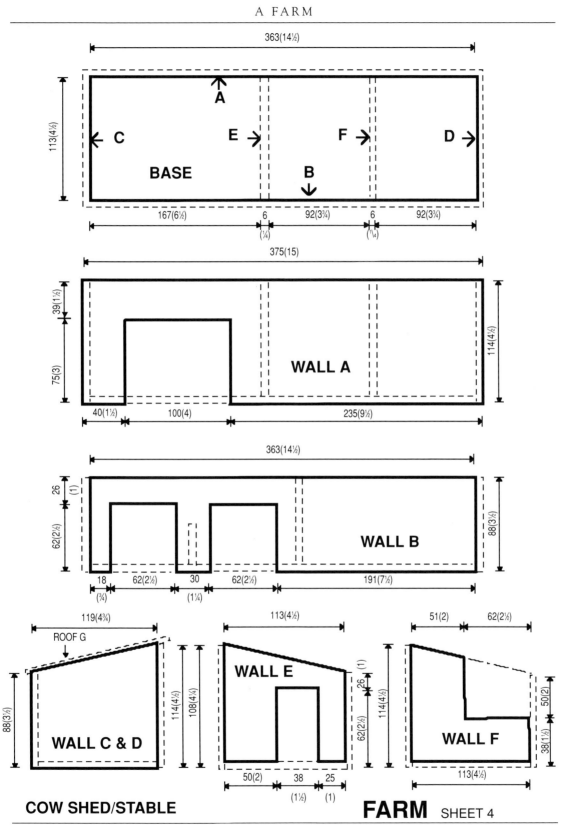

363(14½)

113(4½)

A

C   E   F   D

BASE

B

167(6½)   6 (¼)   92(3¾)   6 (1¼)   92(3¾)

375(15)

39(1½)

75(3)

WALL A

114(4½)

40(1½)   100(4)   235(9½)

363(14½)

26 (1)

62(2½)

WALL B

88(3½)

18 (¾)   62(2½)   30 (1¼)   62(2½)   191(7½)

119(4¾)

ROOF G

88(3½)

114(4½)   108(4¼)

WALL C & D

113(4½)

WALL E

26 (1)

62(2½)

114(4½)

50(2)   38 (1½)   25 (1)

51(2)   62(2½)

50(2)

WALL F

38(1½)

113(4½)

COW SHED/STABLE

FARM SHEET 4

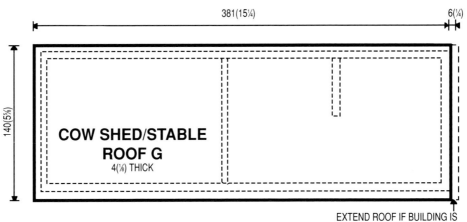

381(15¼)　　6(¼)

140(5⅝)

**COW SHED/STABLE
ROOF G**
4(⅛) THICK

EXTEND ROOF IF BUILDING IS
<u>NOT</u> TO BE FIXED TO BASE

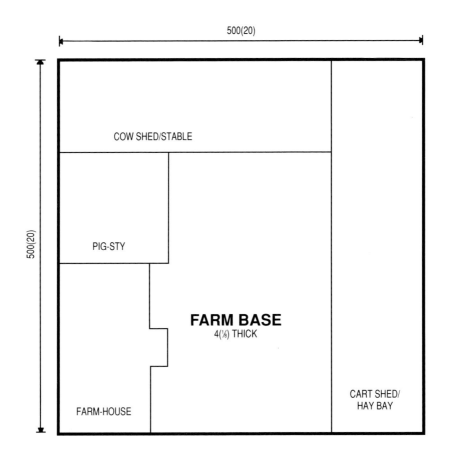

500(20)

500(20)

COW SHED/STABLE

PIG-STY

FARM BASE
4(⅛) THICK

CART SHED/
HAY BAY

FARM-HOUSE

FARM

SHEET 5

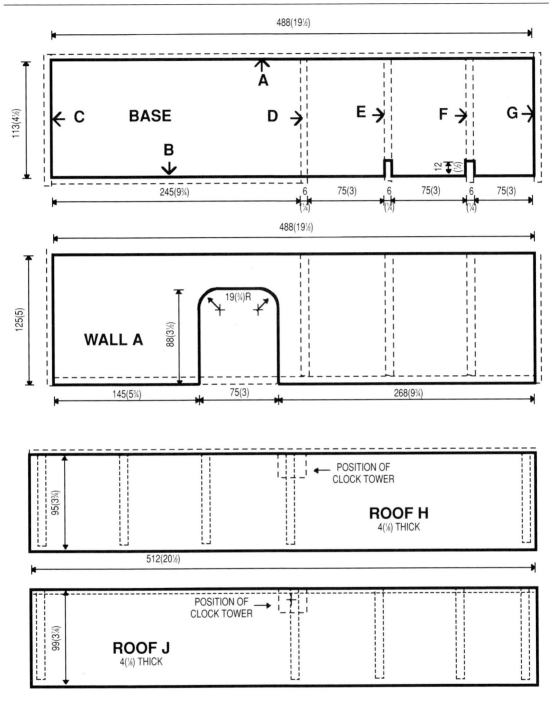

CART SHED/HAY BAY

FARM

SHEET 6

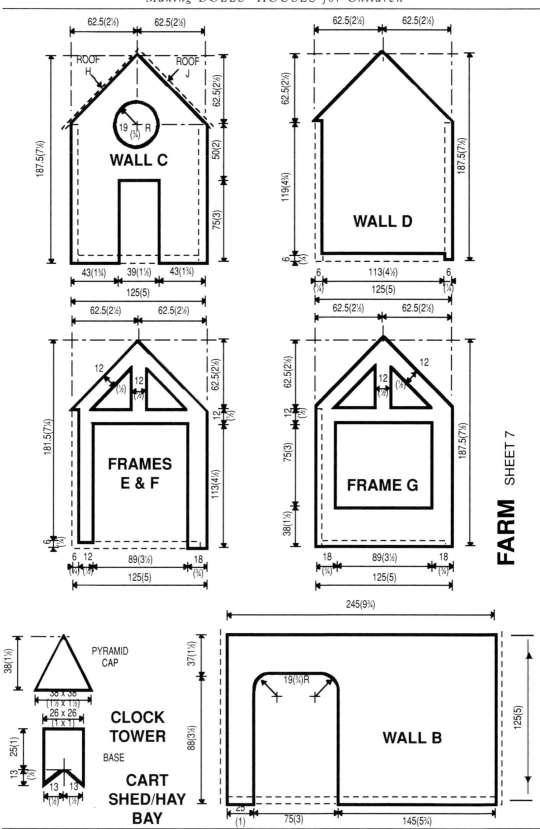

62.5(2½) 62.5(2½)

ROOF H ROOF J

19 (¾) R

WALL C

62.5(2½)

50(2)

75(3)

187.5(7½)

43(1¾) 39(1½) 43(1¾)

125(5)

62.5(2½) 62.5(2½)

62.5(2½)

119(4¾)

6 (¼)

WALL D

187.5(7½)

6 (¼) 113(4½) 6 (¼)

125(5)

62.5(2½) 62.5(2½)

12 (½) 12 (½)

FRAMES E & F

62.5(2½)

12 (½)

113(4½)

181.5(7¼)

6 (¼)

6 12 (¼) (½) 89(3½) 18 (¾)

125(5)

62.5(2½) 62.5(2½)

12 (½) 12 (½)

FRAME G

62.5(2½)

12 (½)

75(3)

38(1½)

187.5(7½)

18 (¾) 89(3½) 18 (¾)

125(5)

FARM SHEET 7

245(9¾)

38(1½)

PYRAMID CAP

38 x 38 (1½ X 1½)

CLOCK TOWER

26 x 26 (1 X 1)

25(1)

13 (½)

13 13 (½) (½)

BASE

CART SHED/HAY BAY

37(1½)

19(¾)R

88(3½)

WALL B

125(5)

25 (1) 75(3) 145(5¾)

126

PROJECT 10

THE CORNER SHOP

T his toy is designed to compliment the Georgian Dolls' House. Its door architrave and cornice are very similar to that of the Georgian house.

Full access to the Shop interior is provided by the two hinged walls which also allow access to the inside of the bay windows for window dressing.

As with the Georgian Dolls' House, use is made of timber mouldings for cornices and architrave. The profile and size of these mouldings need not necessarily be the same as those detailed on the plans but if the sizes do differ, then appropriate amendments must be made to the dimensions of these components as needed to provide a proper fit. The 6 × 6 mm ($\frac{1}{4}$ in × $\frac{1}{4}$ in) rebate in the picture frame moulding is required to fit as an overlap to the 6 mm ($\frac{1}{4}$ in) thick door-lining and shop front fascia.

Furnishings for the Shop are described in Project 11. Two lengths of counter and four shelf units should be adequate for this purpose.

CUTTING LIST

$400 \times 400 \times 12$ mm ($16 \times 16 \times \frac{1}{2}$ in)	plywood
$1200 \times 1200 \times 6$ mm ($48 \times 48 \times \frac{1}{4}$ in)	plywood
$160 \times 70 \times 1.5$ mm ($6\frac{1}{2} \times 2\frac{3}{4} \times \frac{1}{16}$ in)	plywood or card
$12 \times 6 \times 476$ mm ($\frac{1}{2} \times \frac{1}{4} \times 19$ in)	timber fillet
$6 \times 6 \times 924$ mm ($\frac{1}{4} \times \frac{1}{4} \times 40\frac{1}{2}$ in)	timber fillet
$15 \times 15 \times 850$ mm ($\frac{5}{8} \times \frac{5}{8} \times 37$ in)	cavetto moulding
$20 \times 12 \times 1400$ mm ($\frac{3}{4} \times \frac{1}{2} \times 56$ in)	picture frame moulding
6 mm ($\frac{1}{4}$ in) diameter $\times 12$ mm ($\frac{1}{2}$ in)	timber dowel
3 mm ($\frac{1}{8}$ in) diameter $\times 24$ mm (1 in)	timber dowel

ANCILLARIES

3 pairs 25 mm (1 in) brass hinges

CONSTRUCTION DETAILS

1. Mark and cut out the components for the base; roof; walls A, B, C, D, E and F; and the walls D and E parapets. Retain the piece cut out from wall C for the doorway opening.

2. Glue and pin the 12×6 mm ($\frac{1}{2}$ in $\times \frac{1}{4}$ in) and 6×6 mm ($\frac{1}{4}$ in $\times \frac{1}{4}$ in) fillets to the interior faces of walls A and B.

3. Cut a 3 mm ($\frac{1}{8}$ in) chamfer along each inner edge of wall C and glue and pin the 6×6 mm ($\frac{1}{4}$ in $\times \frac{1}{4}$ in) fillet to the interior face leaving a 6 mm ($\frac{1}{4}$ in) space at each end of the fillet.

4. Cut out the door lining piece and glue and pin it to the exterior face of wall C so that it forms a 3 mm ($\frac{1}{8}$ in) overlap to the doorway opening

5. Using the piece cut out of wall C to form the doorway opening complete the cutting of the

door and fanlight. Paint or stain the fanlight and lay it aside to dry.

6. Complete the door by cutting out the panel overlay from 1.5 mm ($\frac{1}{16}$ in) thick plywood or card and glue this to the face of the door leaving a 3 mm ($\frac{1}{8}$ in) margin at each side. Fix one pair of 25 mm (1 in) hinges to the back of the door. Fix a small knob (as detailed on the plans) to the door front. Paint the door and lay it aside to dry.

7. Cut from the picture frame moulding the parts to make the door architrave and glue and pin these around the door lining with the rebate in the moulding overlapping the lining and the mitred ends neatly fitting (note that it will be necessary to amend the dimensions as given on the plans if a different size of moulding is used).

8. Construct the door cornice by firstly fixing the 15×15 mm $\times 122$ mm ($\frac{5}{8}$ in $\times \frac{5}{8} \times 4\frac{3}{4}$ in) timber block to wall C immediately above the door architrave and centred on the door opening. Then cut from the 15×15 mm ($\frac{5}{8} \times \frac{5}{8}$ in) cavetto moulding the pieces to form the cornice and glue and pin these to the front and ends of the block with their mitred ends neatly joined.

9. Glue the fanlight into the top part of the doorway opening in wall C from which it was originally cut, and seated in the rebate formed by the overlapping door lining.

10. Fix the door into its opening in wall C by securing the hinges so that it opens inwards with the door stops formed by the overlap of the door lining.

11. Glue and pin the $6 \times 6 \times 50$ mm ($\frac{1}{4} \times \frac{1}{4} \times 2$ in) blocks to the underside of the roof so that they will form stops to the hinged walls D and E when they are fitted.

12. Glue and screw wall A to the base using 3 No. $\frac{5}{8}$ in × 4 countersunk (c/s) screws.

13. Glue and screw wall B to the base using 3 No. $\frac{5}{8}$ in × 4 c/s screws and pin through B into the end of wall A.

14. Glue and screw wall C to the base using 2 No. $\frac{5}{8}$ in × 4 c/s screws and ensuring that the door swings clear of the floor.

15. Apply glue to the appropriate edges of the roof piece and insert it so that it is seated on the fillets previusly fixed to walls A, B and C. Pin through these walls into the edges of the roof to secure it.

16. Cut a 3 mm ($\frac{1}{8}$ in) chamfer on the inside of one end of the walls D and E parapets. Glue and pin the parapets to the edge of the roof with their chamfered ends glued where they meet the chamfers cut on the sides of wall C and with their other ends pinned to the relevant top edges of walls A and B.

The assembly so far will now be as illustrated in Fig. 19. *This is an opportune time to paint or varnish the interior.*

17. Mark and cut out the components forming each of the two bay windows. Cut 3 mm ($\frac{1}{8}$ in) chamfers on each side (at the back) of the pieces which are fenestrated to represent window panes and on one side edge (at the back) of each of the 13 mm ($\frac{5}{8}$ in) wide blank strips. Assemble each window as follows:

i. Glue and pin the two window brackets to the underside of the window base.

ii. Glue and pin the centre fenestrated piece to the window base.

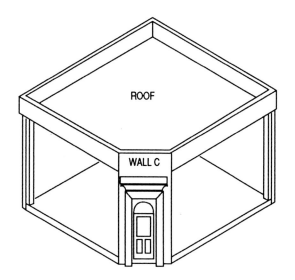

FIGURE 19

iii. Glue and pin one of the splayed fenestrated pieces to the window base with its glued chamfered edge neatly fitting against the chamfered edge of the centre piece.

iv. Repeat instruction iii. for the other splayed fenestrated piece.

v. Glue and pin one of the blank strips to the window base with its glued chamfered edge neatly fitting against the chamfered edge of the splayed fenestrated piece.

vi. Repeat instruction v. for the other blank strip.

vii. Glue and pin the window top to the top edges of the assembled fenestrated and blank pieces. Allow this glued assembly to set firm.

viii. Cut from the cavetto moulding the pieces required to make the window cornice. Glue and pin these to the top of the window assembly with the mitred ends glued and neatly joined.

The completed window assembly will now be as illustrated in Fig. 20. Note that the window base projects 6 mm ($\frac{1}{4}$ in) beyond the back of the assembly. *This is an opportune time to paint or stain the bay windows before they are fixed to the walls.*

18. Cut out the three fascia pieces (note that should the picture frame moulding to form the main cornice be of a different size to that described on the plans it might be necessary to adjust the 36 mm ($1\frac{1}{2}$ in) dimension of the fascias to suit). Carefully cut out the circular pieces which will form catches to secure the hinged walls D and E in their closed positions.

19. Cut a 3 mm ($\frac{1}{8}$ in) chamfer at the back of one end of the fascia to be fixed to wall D parapet. Glue and pin this fascia to the parapet with its bottom edge flush with the bottom edge of the parapet.

20. Repeat instruction 19 to fix the wall E parapet fascia.

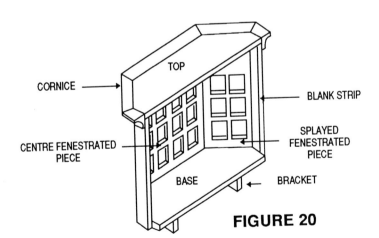

CORNICE — TOP — BLANK STRIP — CENTRE FENESTRATED PIECE — SPLAYED FENESTRATED PIECE — BASE — BRACKET

FIGURE 20

21. Cut 3 mm ($\frac{1}{8}$ in) chamfers at the back of each end of the fascia to be fixed to the top of wall C. Glue and pin this fascia to the wall with its chamfered ends glued and neatly joined to the chamfered ends of the walls D and E parapet fascias.

22. Complete the construction of each of the two retaining catches as follows:

i. Drill a 3 mm ($\frac{1}{8}$ in) diameter hole through the centre of the circular cut-out and countersink it. This is to receiva a $\frac{1}{2}$ in × 4 c/s screw on which the catch will rotate.

ii. Drill a 3 mm ($\frac{1}{8}$ in) diameter hole at the edge of the cut out and into it insert a 12 mm ($\frac{1}{2}$ in) length of 3 mm ($\frac{1}{8}$ in) diameter dowel so that it projects 6 mm ($\frac{1}{4}$ in).

iii. Locate the cut-out into the opening in the fascia from which it was cut out and ensure that it rotates freely. Sand-paper the edges of the cut-out as necessary to ensure a free rotation. When satisfied, mark the position of the centre hole on the parapet to which the fascia is fixed.

iv. Drill a 2 mm ($\frac{3}{32}$ in) diameter hole in the position marked on the parapet and screw the cut-out into its position, again ensuring that it rotates freely.

The completed catch assembly should be as illustrated in Fig. 21.

23. Cut 3 mm ($\frac{1}{8}$ in) chamfers at the back of one end of each of the walls D and E.

24. Secure a bay window assembly into wall D by glueing the contact surfaces and inserting the projection of the window base into the opening so that it seats firmly on the bottom edge of the opening with the window brackets and the sides and top of the window hard against the wall. Pin through the wall into the window and through the window base into the wall.

25. Repeat instruction 24 to fix the bay window into wall E.

26. Cut out the two quoins. A method of forming the grooves to simulate masonry joints is to cut through the face veneer of the plywood along each side of the 'joint' using a sharp trimming knife or fine toothed saw and lift off the strip of veneer between the cuts to form the groove. Clean the groove with the edge of a small file. Glue and pin the quoins in their positions at the one end of walls D and E.

27. Cut out the strips forming the plinths and fix them as follows:
i. Glue and pin the relevant plinth to the bottom of wall A with its left hand end flush

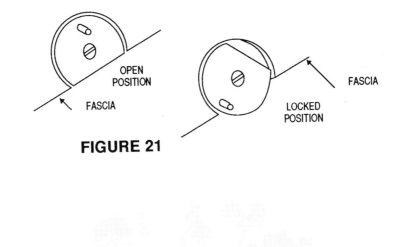

FIGURE 21

with the wall end and the other end about 6 mm ($\frac{1}{4}$ in) short of the wall end to allow clearance for the opening of wall D.

ii.   Glue and pin the relevant plinth to the bottom of wall B with its right hand end overlapping the edge of the wall A plinth and the other end short of the wall end as for the wall A plinth.

iii.   After cutting 3 mm ($\frac{1}{8}$ in) chamfers at the back of the one end of the two short lengths of plinth to be fixed to wall C, glue and pin these plinths to the bottom of the wall, one at each side of the doorway architrave. Note that the chamfered ends should be located at the wall ends – not against the architrave.

iv.   After cutting 3 mm ($\frac{1}{8}$ in) chamfers at the back of the one end of each of the two plinths to be fixed to walls D and E, glue

and pin these plinths to the bottom of these walls with the chamfered ends at the opposite end to the ends where the quoins are fixed.

28. Fix one pair of 25 mm (1 in) hinges to the back of the quoin end of each of walls D and E. With these walls placed in their required positions on the shop front, mark the locations of the hinges on the edges of walls A and B and cut recesses at these positions to receive the hinges which can then be screwed into their positions to secure these walls as access 'doors'. The walls are secured in their closed position by manipulation of the catches described in instruction 22. The chamfered end should meet neatly with the chamfers cut on the sides of wall C.

29. Complete the Corner Shop by application of the desired finish of paint, varnish or patterned paper.

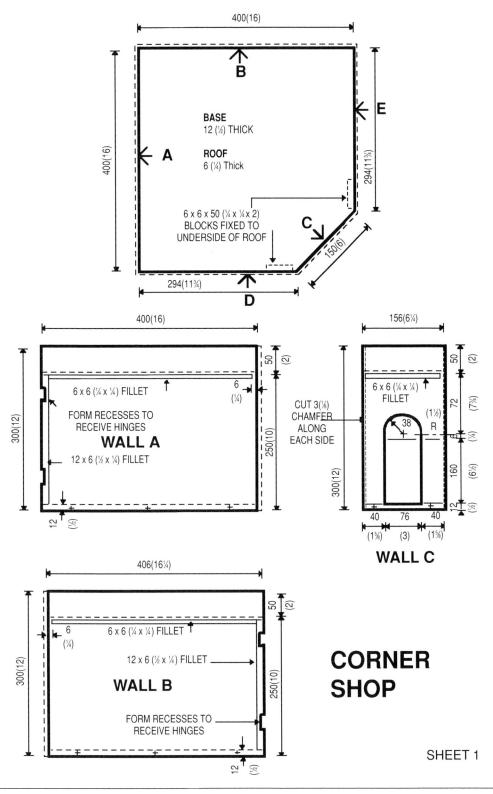

400(16)

400('6)

BASE
12 (½) THICK

ROOF
6 (¼) Thick

B

A

E

294(11¾)

C

150(6)

6 x 6 x 50 (¼ x ¼ x 2)
BLOCKS FIXED TO
UNDERSIDE OF ROOF

294(11¾)

D

400(16)

50 (2)

6
(¼)

6 x 6 (¼ x ¼) FILLET

FORM RECESSES TO
RECEIVE HINGES
WALL A

12 x 6 (½ x ¼) FILLET

300(12)

250(10)

12 (½)

156(6¼)

6 x 6 (¼ x ¼)
FILLET

50 (2)

72 (7¼)

CUT 3(⅛)
CHAMFER
ALONG
EACH SIDE

38

R

(1½)

6 (¼)

160 (6½)

300(12)

12 (½)

40
(1⅝)

76
(3)

40
(1⅝)

WALL C

406(16¼)

300(12)

50 (2)

6
(¼)

6 x 6 (¼ x ¼) FILLET

12 x 6 (½ x ¼) FILLET

WALL B

250(10)

FORM RECESSES TO
RECEIVE HINGES

12 (½)

CORNER SHOP

SHEET 1

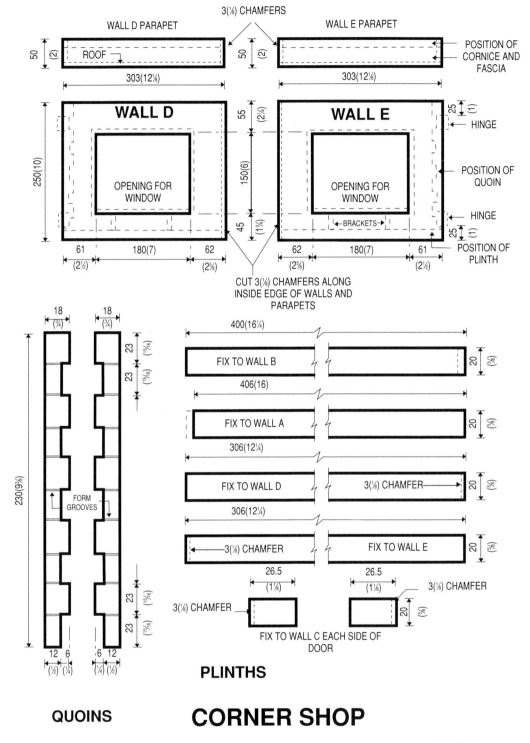

3(⅛) CHAMFERS

WALL D PARAPET

WALL E PARAPET

POSITION OF CORNICE AND FASCIA

ROOF

50 (2)

50 (2)

303(12⅛)

303(12⅛)

WALL D

WALL E

250(10)

55 (2¼)

150(6)

45 (1¾)

OPENING FOR WINDOW

OPENING FOR WINDOW

25 (1)

HINGE

POSITION OF QUOIN

HINGE

BRACKETS

25 (1)

POSITION OF PLINTH

61 (2½)

180(7)

62 (2⅝)

62 (2⅝)

180(7)

61 (2½)

CUT 3(⅛) CHAMFERS ALONG INSIDE EDGE OF WALLS AND PARAPETS

18 (¾)

18 (¾)

23 (¹⁵⁄₁₆)

23 (¹⁵⁄₁₆)

400(16¼)

FIX TO WALL B

20 (⅝)

406(16)

FIX TO WALL A

20 (⅝)

306(12¼)

FIX TO WALL D

3(⅛) CHAMFER

20 (⅝)

230(9⅜)

FORM GROOVES

306(12¼)

3(⅛) CHAMFER

FIX TO WALL E

20 (⅝)

26.5 (1⅛)

26.5 (1⅛)

3(⅛) CHAMFER

23 (¹⁵⁄₁₆)

23 (¹⁵⁄₁₆)

3(⅛) CHAMFER

FIX TO WALL C EACH SIDE OF DOOR

20 (⅝)

12 (½)

6 (¼)

6 (¼)

12 (½)

PLINTHS

QUOINS

CORNER SHOP

SHEET 2

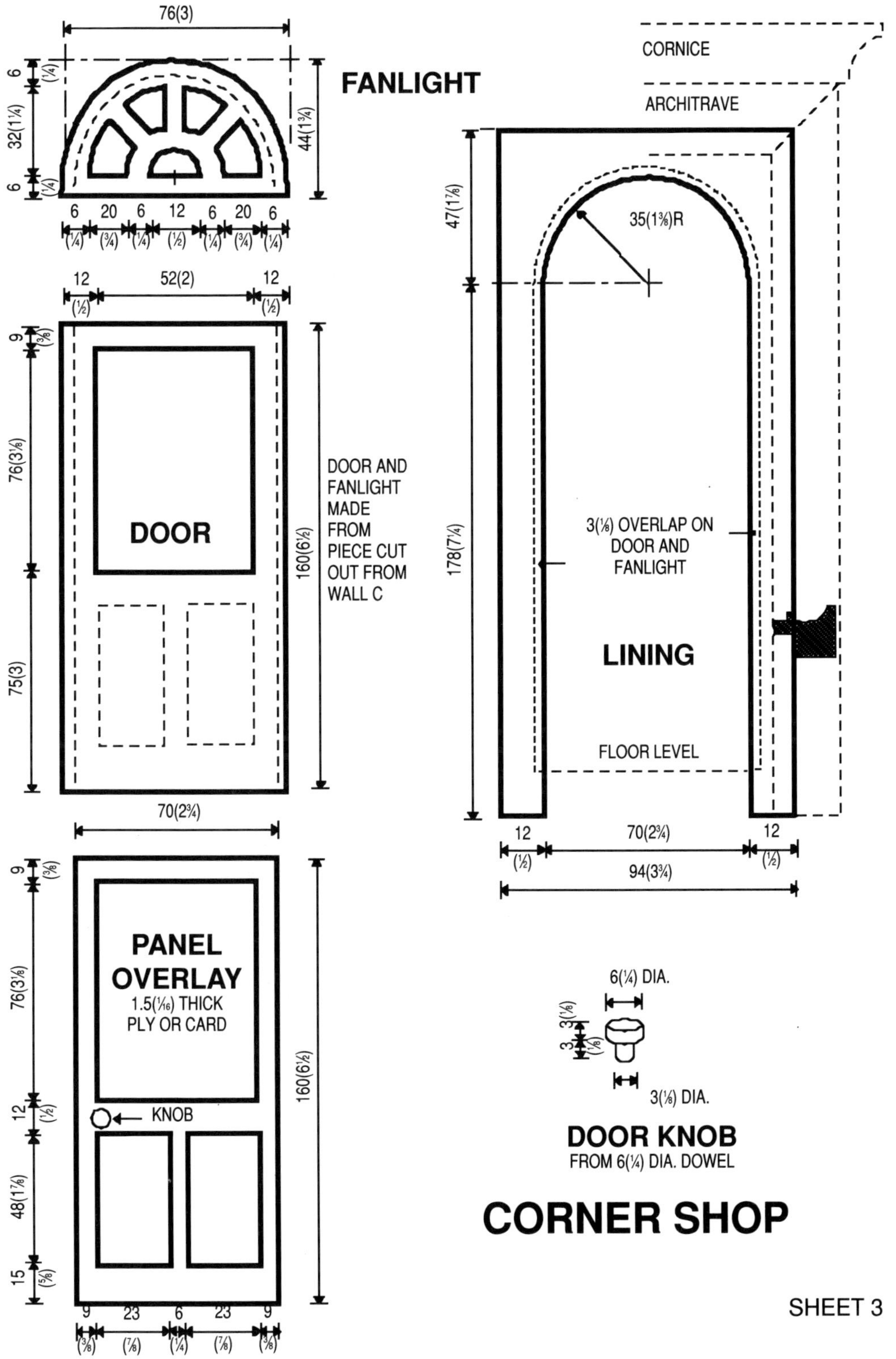
FANLIGHT
76(3)
6 (¼)
32(1¼)
6 (¼)
44(1¾)
6 20 6 12 6 20 6
(¼) (¾) (¼) (½) (¼) (¾) (¼)
12 52(2) 12
(½) (½)
DOOR
9 (⅜)
76(3⅛)
75(3)
160(6½)
DOOR AND FANLIGHT MADE FROM PIECE CUT OUT FROM WALL C
70(2¾)
PANEL OVERLAY
1.5(1/16) THICK PLY OR CARD
KNOB
9 (⅜)
76(3⅛)
12 (½)
48(1⅞)
15 (⅝)
160(6½)
9 23 6 23 9
(⅜) (⅞) (¼) (⅞) (⅜)
CORNICE
ARCHITRAVE
47(1⅞)
35(1⅜)R
178(7¼)
3(⅛) OVERLAP ON DOOR AND FANLIGHT
LINING
FLOOR LEVEL
12 70(2¾) 12
(½) (½)
94(3¾)
6(¼) DIA.
3 (⅛)
3 (⅛)
3(⅛) DIA.
DOOR KNOB
FROM 6(¼) DIA. DOWEL
CORNER SHOP
SHEET 3

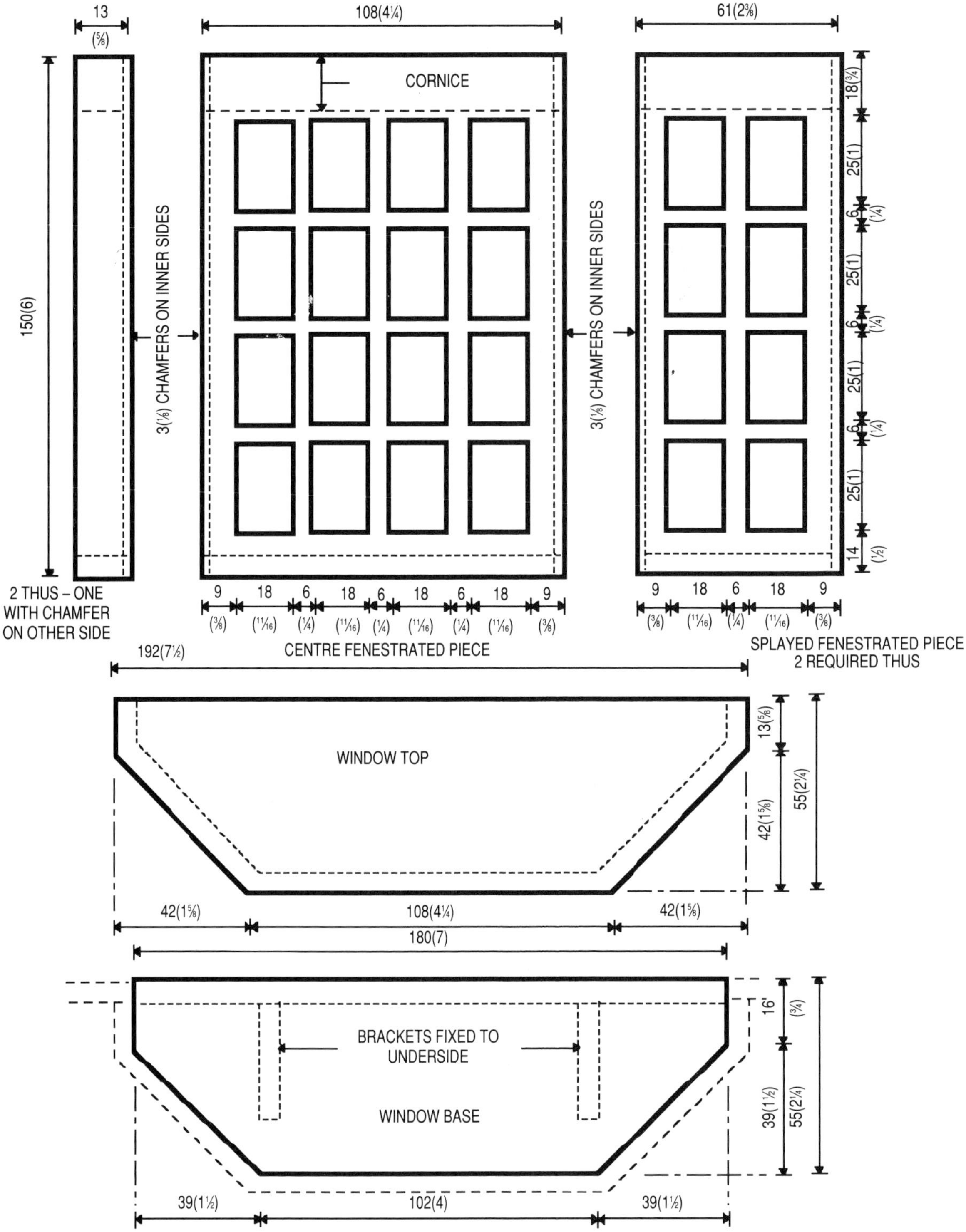
13
(5/8)
108(4¼)
61(2⅜)
CORNICE
150(6)
3(⅛) CHAMFERS ON INNER SIDES
3(⅛) CHAMFERS ON INNER SIDES
18(¾)
25(1)
6
(¼)
25(1)
6
(¼)
25(1)
6
(¼)
25(1)
14
(½)
2 THUS – ONE WITH CHAMFER ON OTHER SIDE
9 18 6 18 6 18 6 18 9
(⅜) (11/16) (¼) (11/16) (¼) (11/16) (¼) (11/16) (⅜)
CENTRE FENESTRATED PIECE
9 18 6 18 9
(⅜) (11/16) (¼) (11/16) (⅜)
SPLAYED FENESTRATED PIECE
2 REQUIRED THUS
192(7½)
WINDOW TOP
13(⅝)
42(1⅝)
55(2¼)
42(1⅝)
108(4¼)
42(1⅝)
180(7)
BRACKETS FIXED TO UNDERSIDE
WINDOW BASE
16
(¾)
39(1½)
55(2¼)
39(1½)
102(4)
39(1½)

BAY WINDOWS 2 SETS REQUIRED THUS **CORNER SHOP** SHEET 4

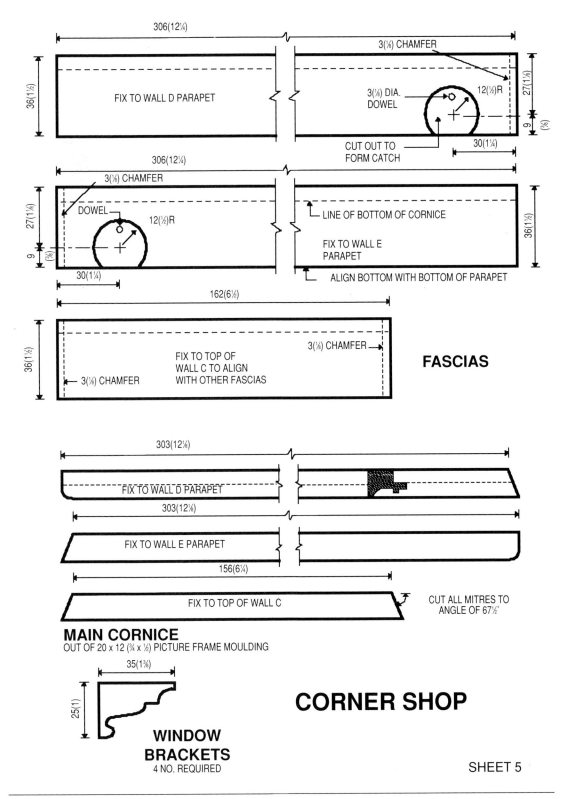

306(12¼)

36(1½)

FIX TO WALL D PARAPET

3(⅛) CHAMFER

3(⅛) DIA.
DOWEL

12(½)R

27(1⅛)

9
(⅜)

CUT OUT TO
FORM CATCH

30(1¼)

306(12¼)

3(⅛) CHAMFER

27(1⅛)

DOWEL

12(½)R

9
(⅜)

30(1¼)

LINE OF BOTTOM OF CORNICE

FIX TO WALL E
PARAPET

36(1½)

ALIGN BOTTOM WITH BOTTOM OF PARAPET

162(6½)

36(1½)

FIX TO TOP OF
WALL C TO ALIGN
WITH OTHER FASCIAS

3(⅛) CHAMFER

3(⅛) CHAMFER

FASCIAS

303(12⅛)

FIX TO WALL D PARAPET

303(12⅛)

FIX TO WALL E PARAPET

156(6¼)

FIX TO TOP OF WALL C

CUT ALL MITRES TO
ANGLE OF 67½°

MAIN CORNICE
OUT OF 20 x 12 (¾ x ½) PICTURE FRAME MOULDING

35(1⅜)

25(1)

**WINDOW
BRACKETS**
4 NO. REQUIRED

CORNER SHOP

SHEET 5

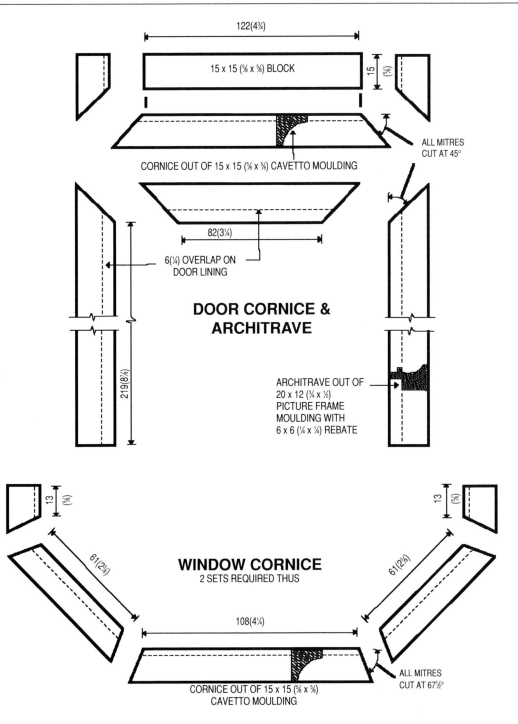

122(4¾)

15 x 15 (⅝ x ⅝) BLOCK

15 (⅝)

ALL MITRES
CUT AT 45°

CORNICE OUT OF 15 x 15 (⅝ x ⅝) CAVETTO MOULDING

82(3¼)

6(¼) OVERLAP ON
DOOR LINING

219(8⅞)

DOOR CORNICE &
ARCHITRAVE

ARCHITRAVE OUT OF
20 x 12 (¾ x ½)
PICTURE FRAME
MOULDING WITH
6 x 6 (¼ x ¼) REBATE

13 (⅝)

13 (⅝)

61(2⅜)

61(2⅜)

WINDOW CORNICE
2 SETS REQUIRED THUS

108(4¼)

ALL MITRES
CUT AT 67½°

CORNICE OUT OF 15 x 15 (⅝ x ⅝)
CAVETTO MOULDING

CORNER SHOP

SHEET 6

PROJECT 11

DOLLS' HOUSE FURNITURE

The range of furniture detailed in this project has been designed to a scale of 1/12 to suit the houses described in the other projects. It is sturdily built to withstand the normal usage to which dolls' house furniture can be expected to be subjected.

All items are made from small pieces and off-cuts of 9 mm ($\frac{3}{8}$ in), 6 mm ($\frac{1}{4}$ in) and 4 mm ($\frac{1}{8}$ in) thick plywood or timber, and for this reason a 'Cutting List' has not been provided.

If a good quality glue is used and a proper pressure is maintained until the glue has achieved a firm bond, no other fixatives should be necessary. However, for convenience, it might be advisable at times to use the glue in conjunction with pin fastenings to secure adjoining pieces and to apply the necessary pressure on the glued joint.

The furniture can be finished in a variety of ways but colourful paints will make it look attractive and also conceal the laminates of the plywood which would otherwise be most noticeable in such small pieces.

It is suggested that suites of furniture can be made up from the items described in this project as follows:

Dining Room suite – the dining room table, 4 chairs, and the dresser.

Lounge suite – 2 armchairs, the settee and coffee table.

Bedroom suite – a single and a double bed, 2 chairs, the dressing table and chest of drawers.

Shop fittings – 2 counter units and 4 shelf units.

CONSTRUCTION DETAILS

Chair

1. Cut out the 4 components required, i.e. the two frame pieces, a seat and a back (the latter 4 mm ($\frac{1}{8}$ in) thick). Note that the two frames can be cut from a single piece, size 76 × 50 mm (3 × 2 ins), as indicated on the plan by the dotted line showing the second frame.

2. Fix one edge of the seat onto its position on one of the frames. It will be helpful to hold the frame in a vice whilst making this fixture.

3. Fix the other edge of the seat onto the other frame.

4. Fix the back onto its position on the two upstands of the frames.

Dining room table

1. Cut out the 3 pieces required, i.e. the top and two pedestal legs.

2. Fix the legs together by sliding the slot cut in one into the slot cut in the other.

3. Fix the top onto the pedestal legs assembly.

Dresser

1. Cut out the 8 pieces required, i.e. the two sids, the work-top C, the base E, the 3 shelves A, B and D, and the back (the latter 4 mm ($\frac{1}{8}$ in) thick).

2. Fix a side to each end of the base.

3. Fix the worktop C onto the 'steps' cut on the sides.

4. Fix the top shelf A between the sides at their top.

5. Secure the back to the assembly of sides, base, worktop and top shelf. This fixture should ensure that the unit is square.

6. Fix the remaining shelves B and D into their locations between the sides.

Armchair and settee

The construction description is the same for both the armchair and the settee. Note that all pieces are cut from 9 mm ($\frac{3}{8}$ in) thick timber.

1. Cut out the 4 pieces required, i.e. the two sides, the back and the seat.

2. Fix the back edge of the seat to the bottom of the back.

3. Fix the assembly of seat and back to one of the sides ensuring that the required angle of incline is obtained.

4. Fix the other side piece to the other side of the assembly.

A pleasing appearance to this particular furniture can be achieved by covering it with a patterned cotton fabric which can be cemented to it using the same PVA adhesive as is used for securing timber joints.

Coffee table

1. Cut out the 4 components required, i.e. the top, the spreader and two legs.

2. Fix the two legs to the spreader by inserting the slots of one into the slots of the others.

3. Fix the top onto the assembly of legs and spreader.

Chest of drawers

1. Cut out the 6 pieces required, i.e. the front and back, the two sides, the top and the base.

2. Fix a side to each end of the base.

3. Fix the front and the back to the assembly of base and sides.

4. Fix the top onto the assembly so far completed.

5. Cut out the 4 drawer fronts from 1.5 mm ($\frac{1}{16}$ in) thick plywood or card and glue them to the face of the front in the positions as dimensioned on the plans.

6. Drill 1.5 mm ($\frac{1}{16}$ in) diameter holes into the drawer fronts and insert in each a short length of similar diameter dowel so that each projects 1.5 mm ($\frac{1}{16}$ in) to represent knobs.

Beds

The construction requirement is the same for both the single and the double beds.

1. Cut out the 3 pieces required, i.e. the base, head and foot.

2. Fix the foot to one end of the base.

3. Fix the head to the other end of the base ensuring that the unit stands square on its four legs.

Dressing table

1. Cut out the 9 pieces required, i.e. the back (4 mm ($\frac{1}{8}$ in) thick), front, top, 4 sides and 2 bases.

2. Fix a side to the two edges of each of the two base pieces,

3. Fix each assembly of a base and two sides to the back of the front piece.

4. Fix the back to the assembly of front, sides and bases ensuring that the assembly is square.

5. Fix the top onto the assembly so far completed.

6. Cut out the 5 drawer fronts from 1.5 mm ($\frac{1}{16}$ in) thick plywood or card and glue them to the face of the front in the positions as dimensioned on the plans.

7. Drill 1.5 mm ($\frac{1}{16}$ in) diameter holes in the drawer fronts and insert in each a short length of similar diameter dowel so that each projects 1.5 mm ($\frac{1}{16}$ in) to represent knobs.

Finish the front of the oval-shaped piece formed on the back with a silver paint to represent the mirror.

Shop counter unit

1. Cut out the 7 pieces required, i.e. the front, top, base, two sides, shelf and divider.

2. Fix a side to each end of the base.

3. Fix the front to the assembly of base and sides.

4. Fix the top to the assembly so far completed.

5. Secure the divider to the shelf by inserting the slot cut in one into the slot in the other, then fix this assembly into the counter unit assembly so far completed.

6. Cut out the 4 panels from 1.5 mm ($\frac{1}{16}$ in) thick plywood or card and glue them to the face of the front in the positions as dimensioned on the plans.

Shop shelf unit

1. Cut out the 9 pieces required, i.e. the two sides, worktop, base, top shelf, two upper shelves, lower shelf and back (the latter 4 mm ($\frac{1}{8}$ in) thick).

2. Fix a side to each end of the base.

3. Fix the worktop onto the 'steps' formed on the sides.

4. Fix the top shelf onto the top edges of the sides.

5. Fix the back to the assembly of sides, base, worktop and top shelf. This fixture should ensure that the unit is square.

6. Complete the unit by fixing the upper and lower shelves into their positions between the sides.

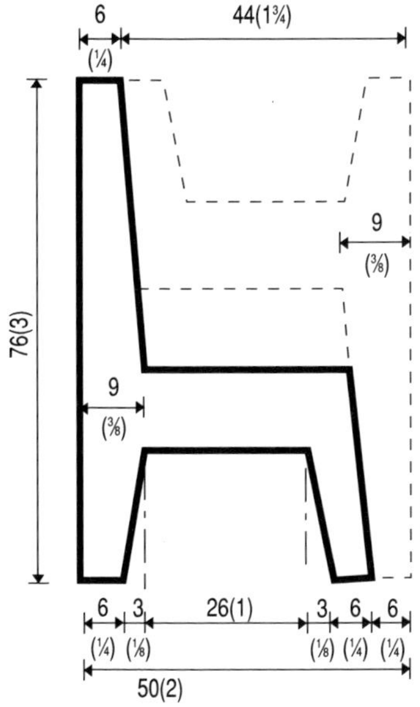
6
(¼)
44(1¾)
76(3)
9
(⅜)
44(1¾)
9
(⅜)
12
(½)
20(¾)
6 3 26(1) 3 6 6
(¼) (⅛) (⅛) (¼) (¼)
50(2)

FRAME
2 REQUIRED THUS

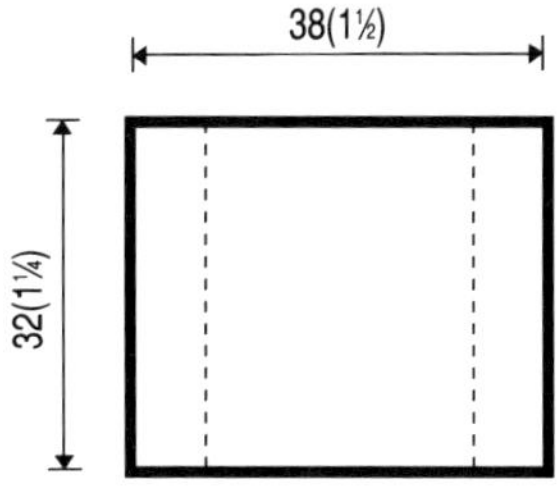
38(1½)
32(1¼)

SEAT

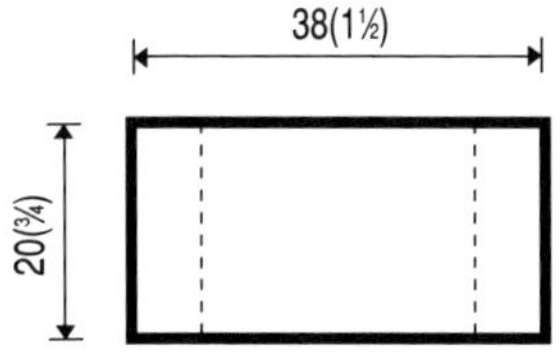
38(1½)
20(¾)

BACK
4(⅛) THICK

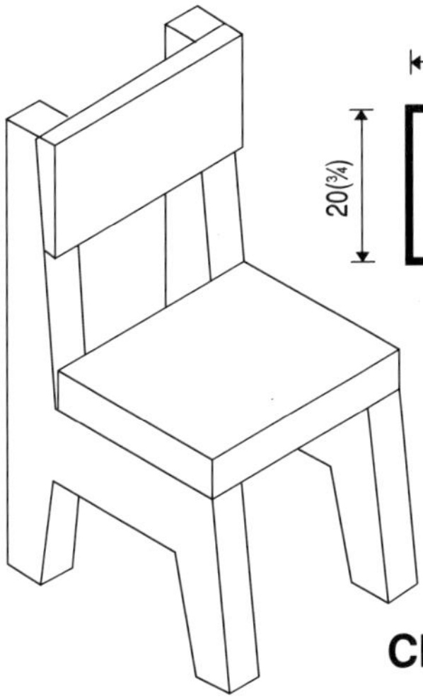

CHAIR

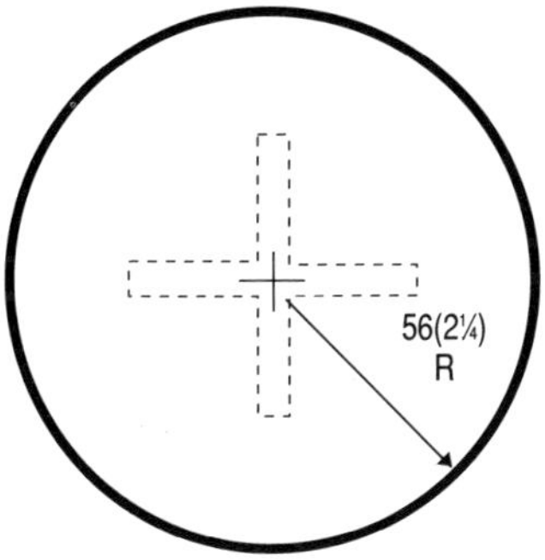
56(2¼)
R

TABLE TOP

DINING ROOM TABLE

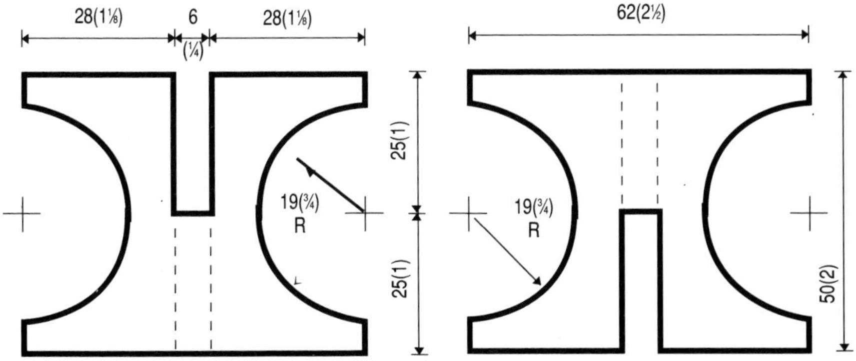
28(1⅛)
6
(¼)
28(1⅛)
19(¾)
R
25(1)
25(1)
62(2½)
19(¾)
R
50(2)

PEDESTAL LEGS

FURNITURE SHEET 1

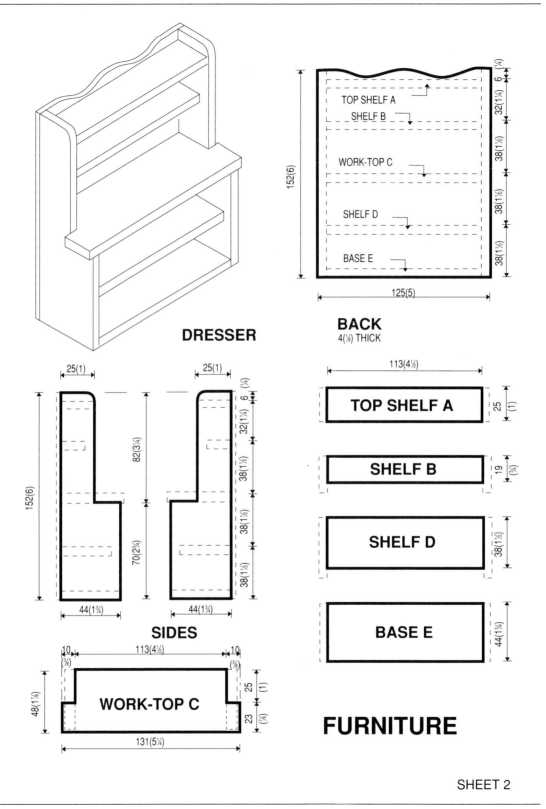

DRESSER

BACK
4(⅛) THICK

SIDES

WORK-TOP C

TOP SHELF A

SHELF B

SHELF D

BASE E

FURNITURE

SHEET 2

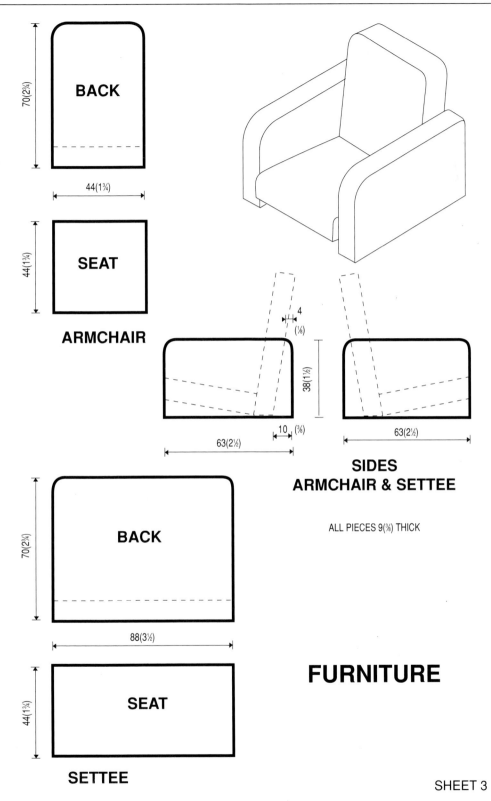

BACK

70(2¾)

44(1¾)

SEAT

44(1¾)

ARMCHAIR

4
(⅛)

38(1½)

10 (⅜)

63(2½)

63(2½)

**SIDES
ARMCHAIR & SETTEE**

ALL PIECES 9(⅜) THICK

BACK

70(2¾)

88(3½)

SEAT

44(1¾)

SETTEE

FURNITURE

SHEET 3

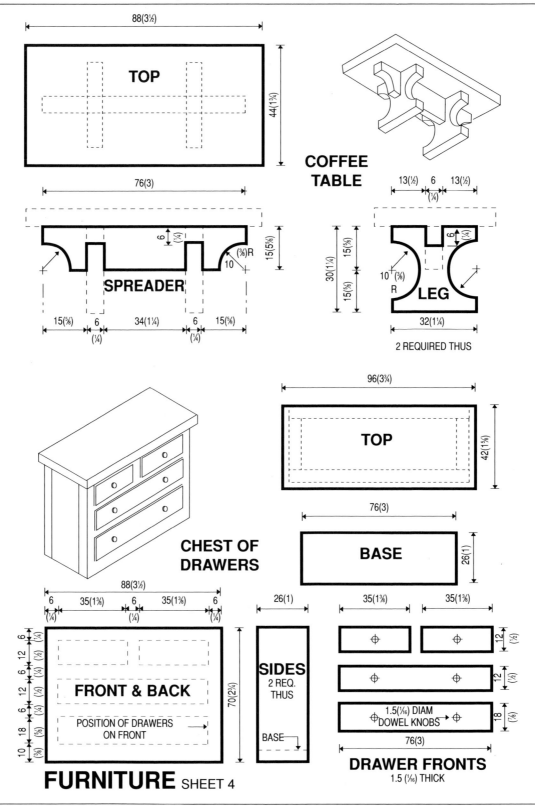

88(3½)

TOP

44(1¾)

COFFEE TABLE

13(½) 6 (¼) 13(½)

76(3)

6 (¼)

15(⅝)

SPREADER

(⅜)R

10

15(⅝) 6 (¼) 34(1¼) 6 (¼) 15(⅝)

30(1¼)

15(⅝)

15(⅝)

6 (¼)

10 (⅜) R

LEG

32(1¼)

2 REQUIRED THUS

96(3¾)

TOP

42(1⅝)

CHEST OF DRAWERS

76(3)

BASE

26(1)

88(3½)

6 (¼) 35(1⅜) 6 (¼) 35(1⅜) 6 (¼)

26(1)

35(1⅜) 35(1⅜)

6 (¼)
12 (½)
6 (¼)
12 (½)
6 (¼)
18 (⅝)
10 (⅜)

FRONT & BACK

POSITION OF DRAWERS ON FRONT

70(2¾)

SIDES
2 REQ. THUS

BASE

12 (½)

12 (½)

1.5(¹⁄₁₆) DIAM
DOWEL KNOBS

18 (⅞)

76(3)

DRAWER FRONTS
1.5 (¹⁄₁₆) THICK

FURNITURE SHEET 4

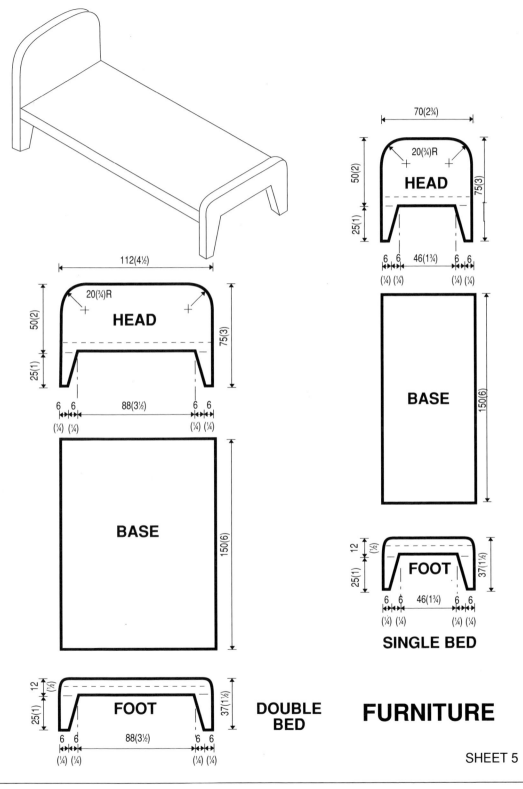

HEAD

70(2¾)

20(¾)R

50(2)

75(3)

25(1)

6 6   46(1¾)   6 6
(¼) (¼)   (¼) (¼)

BASE

150(6)

12 (½)

25(1)

FOOT

37(1½)

6 6   46(1¾)   6 6
(¼) (¼)   (¼) (¼)

SINGLE BED

112(4½)

20(¾)R

HEAD

50(2)

75(3)

25(1)

6 6   88(3½)   6 6
(¼) (¼)   (¼) (¼)

BASE

150(6)

12 (½)

25(1)

FOOT

37(1½)

6 6   88(3½)   6 6
(¼) (¼)   (¼) (¼)

DOUBLE BED

FURNITURE

SHEET 5

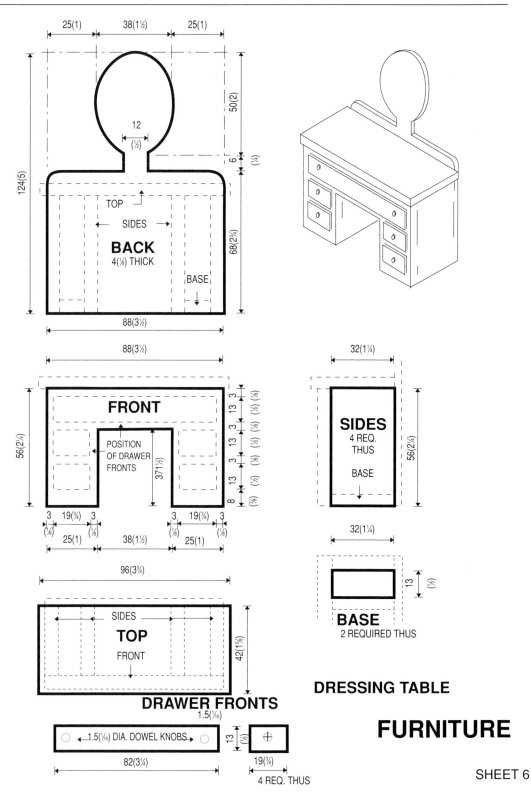

25(1)   38(1½)   25(1)

50(2)

12
(½)

6
(¼)

124(5)

68(2¾)

TOP

SIDES

BACK
4(⅛) THICK

BASE

88(3½)

88(3½)

56(2¾)

FRONT

POSITION
OF DRAWER
FRONTS

371½

3 (⅛)
13 (½)
3 (⅛)
13 (½)
3 (⅛)
13 (½)
8 (⅜)

3   19(¾)   3
(⅛)   (⅛)
25(1)

38(1½)

3   19(¾)   3
(⅛)   (⅛)
25(1)

32(1¼)

SIDES
4 REQ.
THUS

BASE

56(2¾)

32(1¼)

13
(½)

BASE
2 REQUIRED THUS

96(3¾)

SIDES

TOP

FRONT

42(1⅝)

DRAWER FRONTS

1.5(¹⁄₁₆)

←1.5(¹⁄₁₆) DIA. DOWEL KNOBS→

13
(½)

82(3¼)

19(¾)
4 REQ. THUS

DRESSING TABLE

FURNITURE

SHEET 6

148

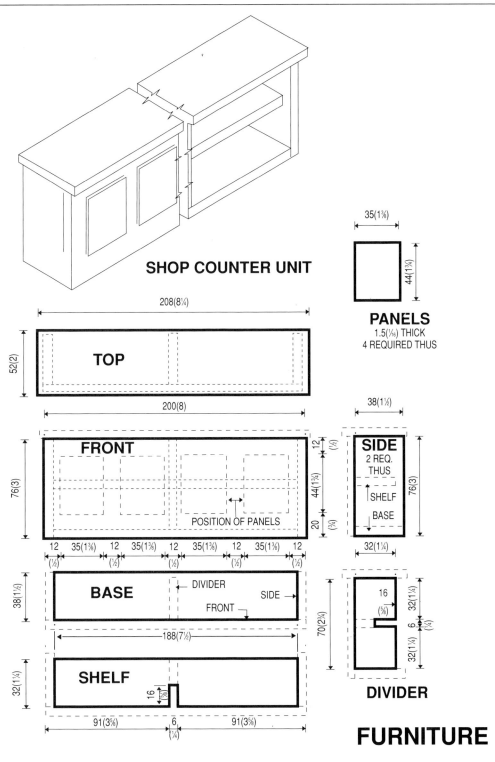

SHOP COUNTER UNIT

PANELS
1.5(1/16) THICK
4 REQUIRED THUS

35(1⅜)

44(1¾)

TOP

208(8¼)

52(2)

FRONT

200(8)

76(3)

12 (½)

44(1¾)

20 (¾)

POSITION OF PANELS

12 (½) 35(1⅜) 12 (½) 35(1⅜) 12 (½) 35(1⅜) 12 (½) 35(1⅜) 12 (½)

SIDE
2 REQ. THUS

38(1½)

76(3)

SHELF

BASE

32(1¼)

BASE

38(1½)

DIVIDER

FRONT

SIDE

70(2¾)

16 (⅝)

6 (¼)

32(1¼)

32(1¼)

DIVIDER

SHELF

188(7½)

32(1¼)

16 (⅝)

91(3⅝) 6 (¼) 91(3⅝)

FURNITURE

SHEET 7

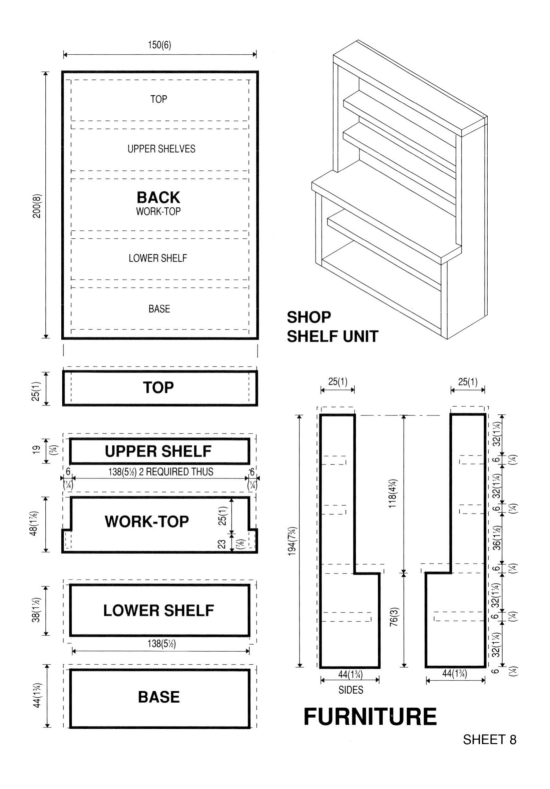

150(6)

200(8)

TOP

UPPER SHELVES

BACK
WORK-TOP

LOWER SHELF

BASE

25(1)

TOP

19 (¾)

UPPER SHELF

6 (¼)   138(5½) 2 REQUIRED THUS   6 (¼)

48(1⅞)

WORK-TOP

25(1)

23 (⅞)

38(1½)

LOWER SHELF

138(5½)

44(1¾)

BASE

**SHOP
SHELF UNIT**

25(1)   25(1)

194(7¾)

118(4¾)

76(3)

32(1¼)
6 (¼)
32(1¼)
6 (¼)
36(1½)
6 (¼)
32(1¼)
6 (¼)
32(1¼)
6 (¼)

44(1¾)   44(1¾)
SIDES

FURNITURE

SHEET 8

PROJECT 12

TUDOR DOLLS' HOUSE

T he style of this toy with its overhanging first floor which is typical of the Tudor period causes it to be rather more complex than any of the previous projects because of the need to manufacture and assemble more components in its construction. For this reason it is the last of the projects in this book and if the reader has progressed through the construction of the previous projects, no real difficulty should be encountered when making this very attractive dolls' house. Its scale is 1/12.

A feature of this toy is a simulated Tudor-style kitchen range with its large, open fireplace. This is just another example of what can be included with the internal fixtures, but the more adventurous craftsperson might wish to improve upon this or even introduce additional features. For example, lengths of fillet can be fixed to the underside of the floors to represent beams. However, the important thing to remember is that thought must be given to how and when such features should be fixed – before, during or after assembly – and when to apply finishes of paint, varnish or patterned paper, or combinations of these.

CUTTING LIST

670 × 288 × 12 mm (26$\frac{3}{4}$ × 11$\frac{1}{2}$ × $\frac{1}{2}$ in)	plywood
1900 × 1200 × 6 mm (75 × 48 × $\frac{1}{4}$ in)	plywood
600 × 400 × 4 mm (24 × 16 × $\frac{1}{8}$ in)	plywood
312 × 100 × 20 mm (12$\frac{1}{2}$ × 4 × $\frac{3}{4}$ in)	timber
510 × 100 × 12 mm (20$\frac{1}{2}$ × 4 × $\frac{1}{2}$ in)	timber
60 × 10 × 10 mm (2$\frac{1}{2}$ × $\frac{3}{8}$ × $\frac{3}{8}$ in)	timber
19 mm ($\frac{3}{4}$ in) diameter × 152 mm (6 in)	timber dowel
12 mm ($\frac{1}{2}$ in) diameter × 100 mm (4 in)	timber dowel
6 mm ($\frac{1}{4}$ in) diameter × 6 mm ($\frac{1}{4}$ in)	timber dowel
6 × 6 × 2600 mm ($\frac{1}{4}$ × $\frac{1}{4}$ × 104 in)	timber fillet

ANCILLARIES

1 pair 25 mm (1 in) brass hinges

2 No. 12 mm ($\frac{1}{2}$ in) diameter wooden balls

CONSTRUCTION DETAILS

1. Mark and cut out the components for the base and walls A, B, C and D.

2. Complete the cutting of the windows using the pieces cut from walls A, C and D to form their openings (*as described in Section 2*). Stain or paint these items and put them aside to dry.

3. Cut out the two parts forming the living room fire-place. Glue and pin the mantlepiece to the top of the 12 mm ($\frac{1}{2}$ in) thick fire-place. Glue and pin this assembly to the inside face of wall A ensuring that a 12mm ($\frac{1}{2}$ in) space is left at the bottom of the wall to clear the base to which the wall will be fixed.

4. Cut out the pieces to form the kitchen range and glue and pin them to the inside face of wall B to complete an assembly as illustrated in the plans. Ensure that a space of 12 mm ($\frac{1}{2}$ in) is left clear at the bottom of the wall (beneath the projecting hearth) to clear the base to which this wall will be fixed.

Suggested finishes for the range are to cover the oven, boiler, back of fireplace and hearth with brick patterned paper, paint the four posts white and clear varnish the chimney breast. An additional touch of realism will be to smudge matt black paint on the back of the fireplace and hearth to simulate blackening from the fire.

5. Glue and pin the 12 mm ($\frac{1}{2}$ in) thick chimney stacks to the outside faces of walls A and B, leaving a 6 mm ($\frac{1}{4}$ in) space at the top of the wall to clear the overhang of the first floor walls.

6. Cut 12 mm ($\frac{1}{2}$ in) wide strips from 4 mm ($\frac{1}{8}$ in) thick plywood. Cut pieces from these strips to the required lengths and glue and pin them around the window openings on the outside faces of walls A, C and D so that they overhang the opening edges 3 mm ($\frac{1}{8}$ in). (*See the 'Arrangement of Half-timbering' illustrations in the plans.*)

7. Glue the windows into the openings from which they were originally cut in walls A, C and D so that they are seated in the rebates formed by the overlap of the strips previously fixed (instruction 6).

8. Commence with the construction of the stair which is in two flights with an intermediate landing. The procedure for its construction is as described in Section 2 and as follows:

i.   Cut out the parts to make the lower flight, i.e. the two 'stepped' sides, the base and the back, and piece U.

ii. Glue and pin the back to one end of the base and similarly fix the sides to the base and the back.

iii. Cut from 4 mm ($\frac{1}{8}$ in) thick plywood the treads (the top one to be 16 mm ($\frac{5}{8}$ in) deep) and risers and fix them onto the 'steps' cut on the side pieces commencing with the bottom riser as described in Section 2.

iv. Glue and pin piece U to the side of the lower flight assembly so that its back vertical edge aligns with the back edge of the stair flight.

v. Cut out the parts to make the upper flight, i.e. the sides and the soffit (note the requirement to cut a 4 mm ($\frac{1}{8}$ in) chamfer at each end of the soffit piece), and piece V.

vi. Glue and pin the sides to the soffit.

vii. Cut out the treads and rises (the top riser 10 mm ($\frac{3}{8}$ in) deep) and fix these onto the 'steps' cut on the side pieces (note that a 6 mm ($\frac{1}{4}$ in) space is left below the bottom riser into which will fit an edge of the landing).

viii Glue and pin V to the side of the upper flight assembly so that its bottom inclined edge aligns with the underside of the soffit.

Lay aside the completed assemblies of the upper and lower stair flights to be fixed into their positions at a later stage.

9. Cut out piece N and retain the piece cut out to form the door opening. Using this piece, fix to it one pair of 25 mm (1 in) brass hinges and a door knob (made as illustrated in the plans for Project 10, the Corner Shop). Paint or stain the door and when dry, secure it by its hinges into the opening in piece N from which it was cut, so that it will open inwards.

10. Glue and pin piece N (with the door) to the back of the lower stair flight. The inside face of piece U which is fixed to this flight should align with an edge of the balustrade upstand on piece N.

11. Cut out the stair landing and glue and pin it to the top edge of piece N. The balustrade upstand on piece N should fit into the recess cut in the landing.

12. Glue and pin the upper stair flight assembly to piece N in its position above the door. The inside face of piece V which is fixed to this flight

should align with an edge of the balustrade upstand on piece N, and the edge of the landing should fit in the space left below the lower riser.

13. Cut out piece P and the small shelf piece. Glue the shelf into the arched niche in cut piece P. Glue and pin this assembly of piece P and shelf to the face of piece N on the opposite side to the stair. Note that the arched door opening in piece P will overhang the sides of the door opening in piece N by 3 mm ($\frac{1}{8}$ in) to form the door stops.

14. Cut out walls L and M, and the first floor.

15. Glue and pin 6 × 6 mm ($\frac{1}{4}$ × $\frac{1}{4}$ in) fillets around the perimeter of the first floor, on its underside and where it will abut walls E, F, G and H. This fillet should be flush with the edges of the floor.

16. Glue and pin a 55 mm ($2\frac{1}{8}$ in) length of 6 × 6 mm ($\frac{1}{4}$ × $\frac{1}{4}$ in) fillet to each of the stair facing sides of walls L and M in the correct position to support the stair landing as indicated on the plans.

17. Glue and pin wall M to the side of the lower stair flight so that the landing is seated on the fillet fixed to this wall for this purpose. Ensure that the back edge of the landing will be in line to abut the face of wall C. Pin through wall M into the edges of pieces N and P.

18. With wall L held in its correct position against the upper stair flight check that the first floor can slide into its position within the slots cut into the walls L and M, and in the floor itself. Adjust as necessary to ensure that this can be achieved and when satisfied, glue these components into place and pin through wall L into the side of the upper stair flight and into the edges of pieces N and P.

19. Cut out the balustrade piece W. Glue and pin it to the edge of piece V at the top of the upper stair flight and pin into its edge through wall M.

This is an opportune time to apply the desired finishes to the insides of walls A, B, and D and to the completed assembly of walls L and M with the stair and first floor. Try to keep the finish material off the surfaces which will be in glued contact.

20. Glue and screw wall C to the base using 3 No $\frac{5}{8}$ in $\times$ 4 countersunk (c/s) screws. Ensure that a 6 mm ($\frac{1}{4}$ in) space is left at the end where it will abut wall M to allow this wall to fit.

21. Glue and screw wall A to the base using 2 No $\frac{5}{8}$ in $\times$ 4 c/s screws and pin through it into the edge of wall C.

22. Glue and screw wall B to the base using 2 No $\frac{5}{8}$ in $\times$ 4 c/s screws.

23. Glue and screw wall D to the base using 2 No $\frac{5}{8}$ in $\times$ 4 c/s screws and pin through it into the edge of wall B.

24. Glue along the top edges of walls A, B, C and D and the contact edges of walls L and M. Lower the assembly of walls L and M with the stair and first floor into position on the base and within walls A, B, C and D. The fillet fixed around the edge of the first floor should be located outside and against the top edges of these walls. Pin through the floor into the tops of walls A, B, C and D, and through wall C into the edge of wall L. Pin through wall D into the edge of wall M, and through wall M into the edge of wall C. Screw from below and through the base into the base of the lower stair flight using a $\frac{3}{4}$ in $\times$ 6 c/s screw.

25. Cut out piece T and glue and pin to its underside a length of 6 $\times$ 6 mm ($\frac{1}{4} \times \frac{1}{4}$ in) fillet. Glue and pin this piece to the top of wall C between walls L and M so that it overhangs with the fillet against the top of the outer face of wall C.

26. Mark and cut out walls E, F, G and H, and the attic floor.

27. Complete the cutting of the windows using the pieces cut from walls E, F, G and H to form their openings (*as described in Section 2*). Stain or paint these items and put them aside to dry.

28. Cut out the parts for the two bedroom fireplaces and fix them to the inside faces of walls E and F as described for the living room fireplace (*instruction 3*). The 12 mm ($\frac{1}{2}$ in) space is left at the bottom to clear the first floor.

29. Glue and pin lengths of 6 $\times$ 6 mm ($\frac{1}{4} \times \frac{1}{4}$ in) fillet to the inside faces of walls E, F, G and H to support the attic floor. Note the requirement to leave spaces at the ends of some of these fillets to clear other walls and/or fillets.

30. Glue and pin wall G to the edge of the first floor and piece T so that its bottom edge is flush with the bottom of the fillets fixed to the underside of the floor and piece T. Pin through wall M into the edge of wall G.

31. Glue and pin wall E to the edge of the first floor with its bottom edge positioned as for wall G and in alignment with it. Pin through wall E into the edge of wall G.

32. Glue and pin wall F to the edge of the first floor with its bottom edge flush with the bottom of the fillet fixed to the underside of the floor.

33. Cut out piece Q. Fix it to the back end of wall H by glueing and pinning into it through wall H. This piece closes the gap which would otherwise be left between the end of wall H and wall G.

34. Glue and pin wall H, with piece1 Q to the edge of the first floor with its bottom edge positioned as for wall F and in alignment with it. Pin through wall H into the edges of walls M and F, and through wall G into piece Q.

35. Cut out pieces R and S (roof supports). Fix piece R to the top surface of the attic floor in its correct position (see plans) by pinning from below and through the floor into its bottom edge. Fix piece S to the top surface of the attic floor in its correct position against piece R. Secure it to the floor as for piece R and pin through piece R into its edge.

This is an opportune time to apply the desired finishes to the inside faces of walls E, F, G and H, and to the underside of the attic floor before proceeding with further assembly.

36. Glue the contact edges of the attic floor and lower it into its position seated on the fillets fixed to walls E, F G and H, and on the tops of walls L and M. Pin through walls E, F, G and H into the edge of the floor, and through the floor into the tops of walls L and M.

37. Cut out pieces J and K and fix them in their correct positions at each end at the back by glueing and pinning them to the edges of the base, and the first and attic floors. Pin through walls A and E into the edges of piece J, and through walls B and F into the edges of piece K.

38. Mark and cut out the roof components X, Y, Z(1) and (Z)2. Cut the required chamfers on roofs Y, Z(1) and Z(2). Also at this stage cut out the 18 mm ($\frac{3}{4}$ in) thick bases for the two chimneys.

39. Glue and fix roof X into its position. Pin through it into the gable edge of wall E, and into piece R. Note that this roof overhangs the gable 12 mm ($\frac{1}{2}$ in).

40. Glue and screw the small chimney base onto its correct position on roof Y (see plans) using a $\frac{5}{8}$ in × 4 c/s screw. Glue and fix this roof into its position and pin through it into the gable edge of wall E, piece R, and the edge of roof X along its ridge. Note that the notch in the chimney base should seat neatly onto roof X.

41. Glue and fix roof Z(2) into its position ensuring that its chamfered edge neatly abuts against the slope of roof X and that it overhangs the gable wall 12 mm ($\frac{1}{2}$ in). Pin through this roof into the gable edge of wall H and into roof X.

42. Glue and screw the larger chimney base onto its correct position on roof Z(1) (see plans) using 2 No $\frac{5}{8}$ in × 4 c/s screws. Glue and fix this roof into its position ensuring that its chamfered edge at the hip neatly adjoins the chamfered hip of roof Y. Pin through roof Z(1) into the gable edge of wall H, piece S, and the edge of roof Z(2) along its ridge. Note that it will be necessary to cut a short length of chamfer on roof Z(1) where it abuts piece R near its apex.

43. Cut out the remaining components to complete the chimneys. Glue and pin the small chimney capping to the top of this chimney. Thought should be given to the desired finishes before assembling the larger chimney. If brick patterned paper is to be used this should be applied to the two pieces of dowel at this stage. Secure the two pieces of dowel to the top surface of the lower capping by glueing and screwing from below the capping up into the dowels using 2 No $\frac{3}{4}$ in × 4 c/s screws. In a similar manner secure the top 6 mm ($\frac{1}{4}$ in) thick capping to the tops of the dowels using 2 No $\frac{3}{4}$ in × 4 c/s screws.. Glue and pin the assembly of dowels and cappings to the top of the chimney base which is fixed to roof Z(1). Complete the assembly by glueing and pinning the 4 mm ($\frac{1}{8}$ in) thick capping to the top of the chimney, and glue the dowel chimney pots into the holes cut in the cappings.

Before proceeding with the fixing of the half-timbering it is recommended that their positions be marked onto the walls (referring to the arrangement illustrated in the plans) and paint the wall surfaces which will remain exposed (recommended colour 'off white').

44. Cut 12 mm ($\frac{1}{2}$ in) wide strips from 4 mm ($\frac{1}{8}$ in) thick plywood. Stain or paint these as desired before fixing. Cut the strips to the correct shape and length and glue them into position. Commence with the timbering in each of the two gables, then the horizontal lengths at the base of the first floor walls, and then the vertical strips at the sides of the window openings ensuring that these strips overhang the openings 3 mm ($\frac{1}{8}$ in). Continue with the remaining vertical strips before completing with the horizonal infil strips, again ensuring that those above and below the window openings overhang 3 mm ($\frac{1}{8}$ in).

45. Glue the windows into the openings from which they were originally cut in walls E, F, G and H so that they are seated in the rebates formed by the overlap of the half-timbering strips previously fixes (*see instruction 44*).

46. Cut out the four pieces to form the barge-boards. Glue and pin them into their positions against the roof edges above the two gables.

47. Cut to shape from 10 × 10 mm ($\frac{3}{8} \times \frac{3}{8}$ in) timber the two short posts to form the finials

and glue and pin them to the gable barge-boards at their apex. Note that the shaped notches cut into the back of these posts should fit neatly over the barge-boards where they meet at their apex.

48. Complete the finials by glueing and pinning a 12 mm ($\frac{1}{2}$ in) diameter wooden ball onto the top of each post. Slightly flatten the surface of the balls where they will sit on the posts.

49. Using strips of 4 mm ($\frac{1}{8}$ in) thick plywood as used for the half timbering (*instruction 44*) cut pieces from them to the required shapes and lengths and glue and pin them to the roof ridges and hips.

50. Complete the house by applying the desired finishes. The toy illustrated in the photograph has been finished with a brick patterned paper on the ground floor walls and on the chimneys. The first floor walls are finished as described in the preamble to instruction 44. The roofs and windows have been finished with a clear varnish.

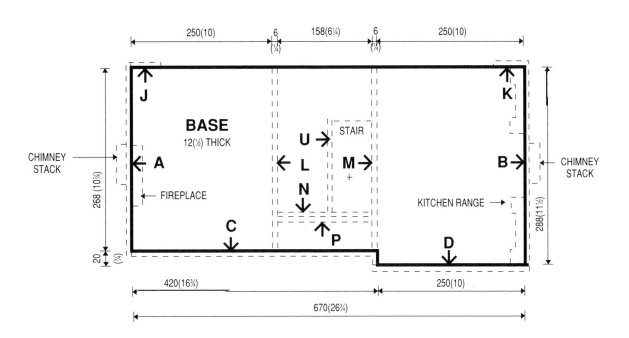

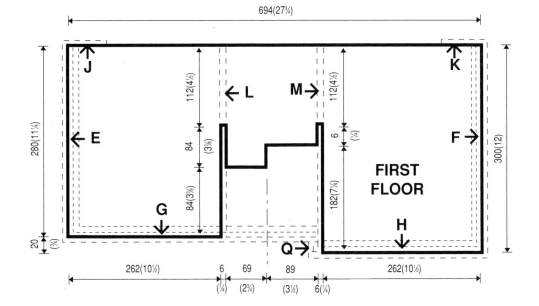

TUDOR DOLLS' HOUSE

SHEET 1

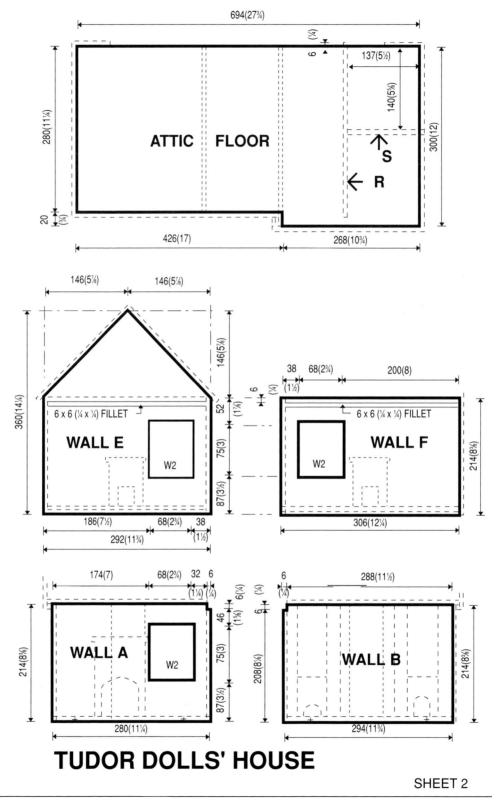

TUDOR DOLLS' HOUSE

SHEET 2

TUDOR
DOLLS' HOUSE

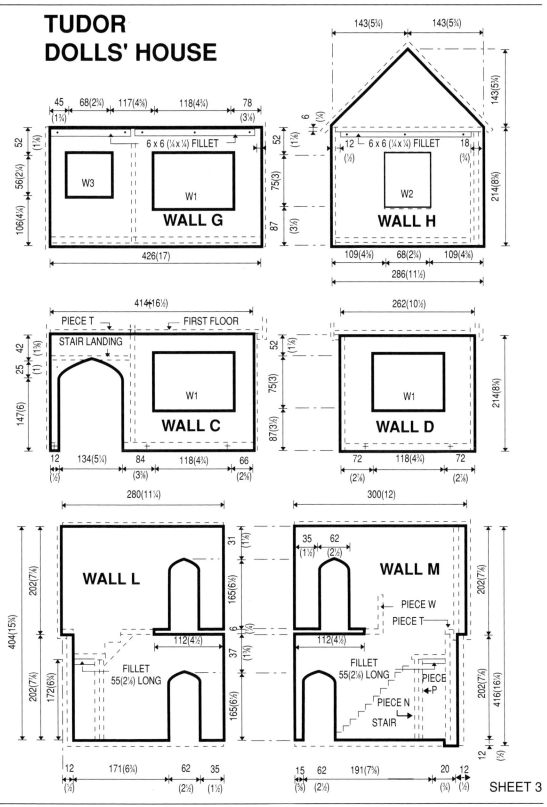

WALL G

WALL H

WALL C

WALL D

WALL L

WALL M

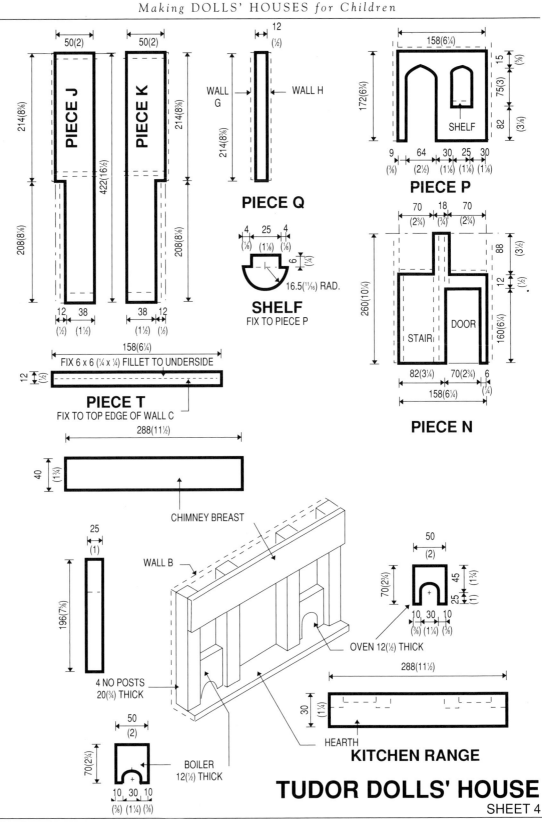

50(2)

PIECE J

214(8⅜)

422(16½)

208(8⅛)

12 (½)   38 (1½)

50(2)

PIECE K

214(8⅜)

208(8⅛)

38 (1½)   12 (½)

12 (½)

WALL G

214(8⅜)

WALL H

PIECE Q

4 (⅛)   25 (1⅛)   4 (⅛)

6 (¼)

16.5 (¹¹⁄₁₆) RAD.

SHELF
FIX TO PIECE P

158(6¼)
FIX 6 x 6 (¼ x ¼) FILLET TO UNDERSIDE

12 (½)

PIECE T
FIX TO TOP EDGE OF WALL C

158(6¼)

172(6¾)

15 (⅝)

75(3)

82 (3⅜)

SHELF

9 (⅜)   64 (2½)   30 (1⅛)   25 (1⅛)   30 (1⅛)

PIECE P

70 (2¾)   18 (¾)   70 (2¾)

88 (3½)

12 (½)

260(10¼)

160(6¼)

STAIR   DOOR

82(3¼)   70(2¾)   6 (¼)

158(6¼)

PIECE N

288(11½)

40 (1¾)

CHIMNEY BREAST

WALL B

25 (1)

196(7⅞)

4 NO POSTS
20(¾) THICK

50 (2)

70(2¾)

BOILER
12(½) THICK

10 (⅜)   30 (1¼)   10 (⅜)

50 (2)

70(2¾)   45 (1¾)

25 (1)

10 (⅜)   30 (1¼)   10 (⅜)

OVEN 12(½) THICK

288(11½)

30 (1¼)

HEARTH

KITCHEN RANGE

TUDOR DOLLS' HOUSE
SHEET 4

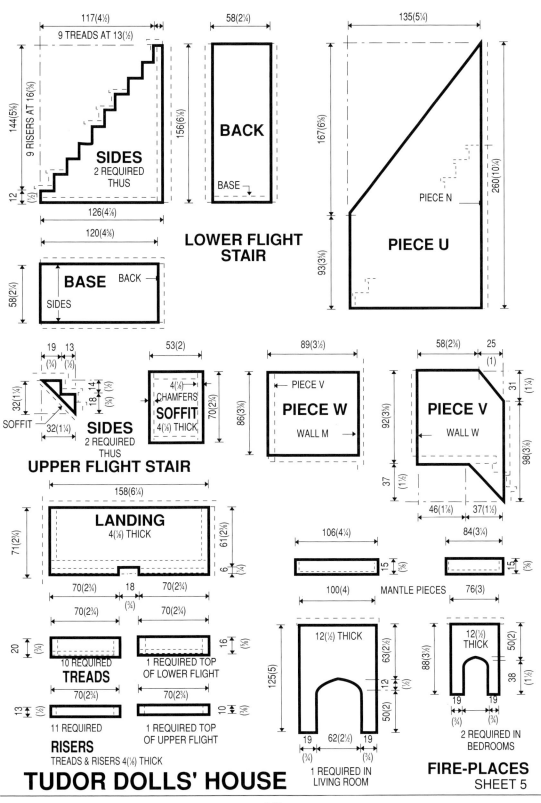

117(4½)
9 TREADS AT 13(½)
144(5⅝)
9 RISERS AT 16(⅝)
12 (½)
126(4⅞)

SIDES
2 REQUIRED
THUS

156(6⅛)

58(2¼)

BACK

BASE

**LOWER FLIGHT
STAIR**

120(4⅝)
58(2¼)

BASE
BACK
SIDES

135(5¼)
167(6⅝)
260(10¼)
PIECE N
93(3⅝)

PIECE U

19 (¾)
13 (½)
32(1¼)
18 14 (¾)(½)
SOFFIT
32(1¼)

SIDES
2 REQUIRED
THUS

UPPER FLIGHT STAIR

53(2)
4(⅛)
CHAMFERS
SOFFIT
4(⅛) THICK
70(2¾)

86(3⅜)
89(3½)
PIECE V
PIECE W
WALL M

58(2⅜) 25 (1)
31 (1¼)
92(3⅝)
PIECE V
WALL W
98(3⅞)
37 (1½)
46(1⅞) 37(1½)

158(6¼)
LANDING
4(⅛) THICK
71(2¾)
61(2⅜)
6 (¼)
70(2¾) 18 (¾) 70(2¾)
70(2¾) 70(2¾)

20 (¾)
16 (⅝)
10 REQUIRED
TREADS
1 REQUIRED TOP
OF LOWER FLIGHT

70(2¾)
13 (½)
70(2¾)
10 (⅜)
11 REQUIRED
1 REQUIRED TOP
OF UPPER FLIGHT

RISERS
TREADS & RISERS 4(⅛) THICK

106(4¼) 15 (⅝)
84(3¼) 15 (⅝)
MANTLE PIECES

100(4)
12(½) THICK
63(2½)
125(5)
12 (½)
50(2)
19 62(2½) 19
(¾) (¾)
1 REQUIRED IN
LIVING ROOM

76(3)
12(½) THICK
88(3½)
50(2)
38 (1½)
19 19
(¾) (¾)
2 REQUIRED IN
BEDROOMS

TUDOR DOLLS' HOUSE

FIRE-PLACES
SHEET 5

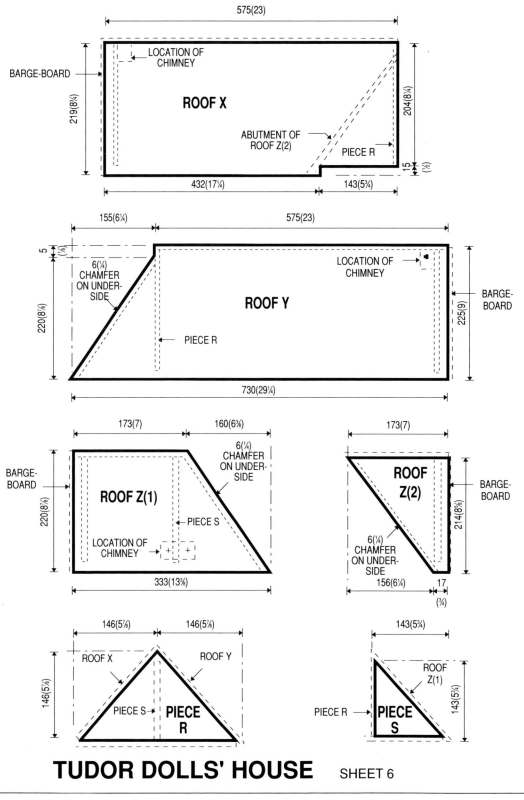

TUDOR DOLLS' HOUSE   SHEET 6

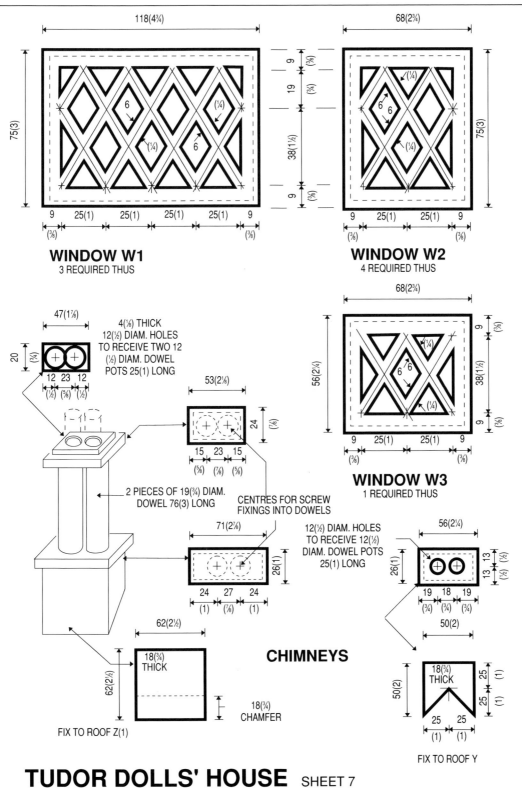

WINDOW W1
3 REQUIRED THUS

WINDOW W2
4 REQUIRED THUS

WINDOW W3
1 REQUIRED THUS

4(⅛) THICK
12(½) DIAM. HOLES
TO RECEIVE TWO 12
(½) DIAM. DOWEL
POTS 25(1) LONG

2 PIECES OF 19(¾) DIAM.
DOWEL 76(3) LONG

CENTRES FOR SCREW
FIXINGS INTO DOWELS

12(½) DIAM. HOLES
TO RECEIVE 12(½)
DIAM. DOWEL POTS
25(1) LONG

CHIMNEYS

18(¾)
THICK

18(¾)
CHAMFER

FIX TO ROOF Z(1)

18(¾)
THICK

FIX TO ROOF Y

TUDOR DOLLS' HOUSE SHEET 7

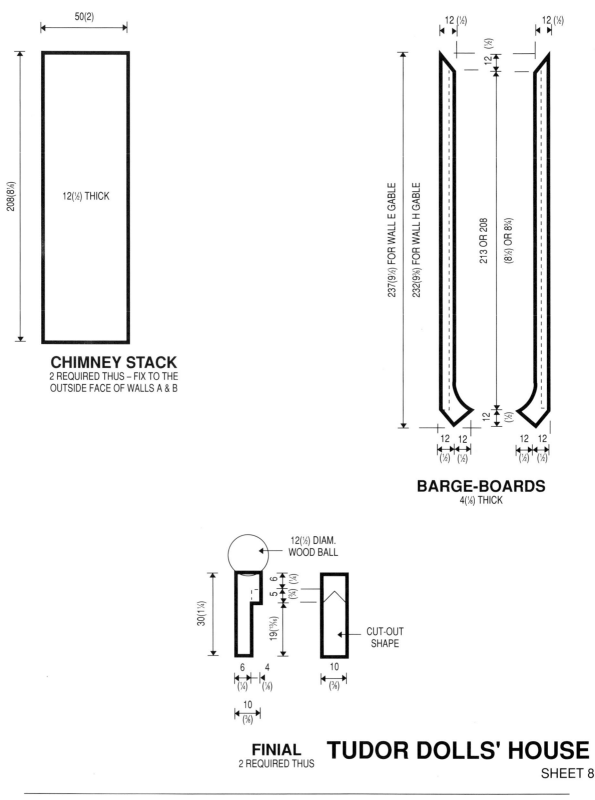

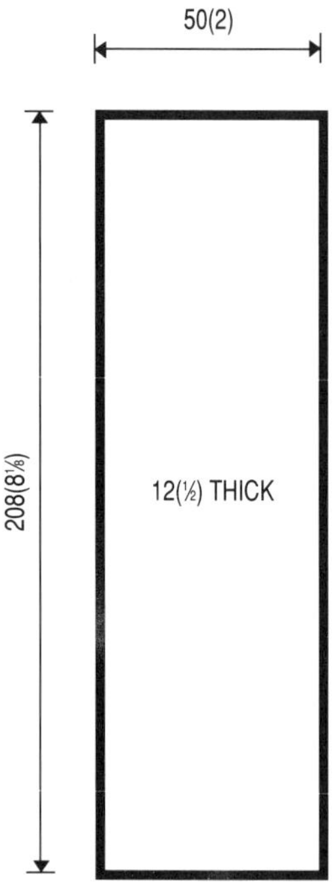
50(2)
208(8⅛)
12(½) THICK

CHIMNEY STACK
2 REQUIRED THUS – FIX TO THE OUTSIDE FACE OF WALLS A & B

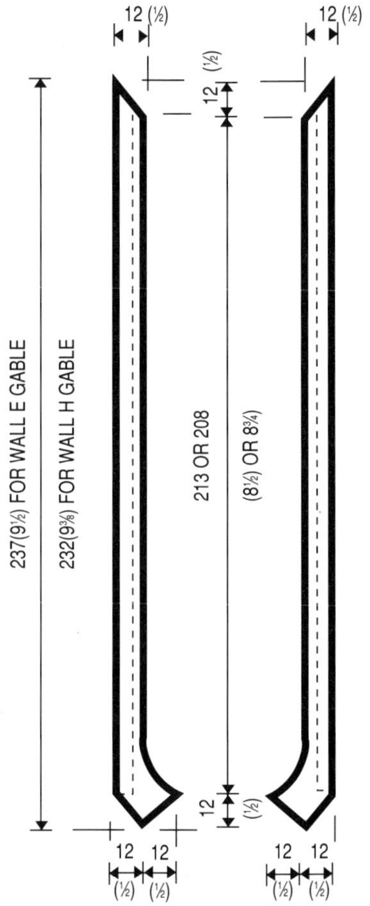
12 (½)
12 (½)
12 (½)
237(9½) FOR WALL E GABLE
232(9⅛) FOR WALL H GABLE
213 OR 208
(8½) OR 8¾)
12 (½)
12 12
(½) (½)
12 12
(½) (½)

BARGE-BOARDS
4(⅛) THICK

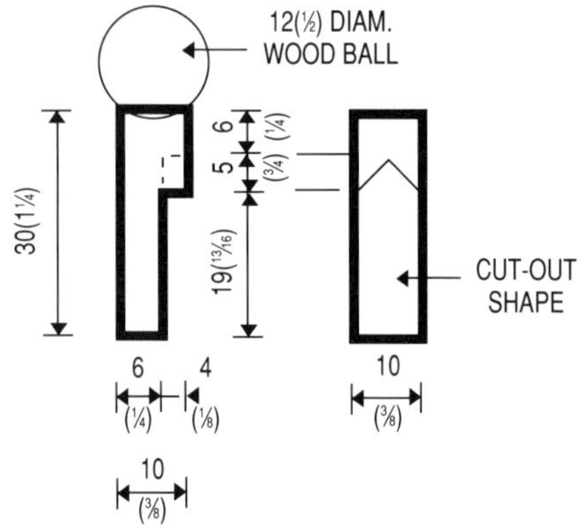
12(½) DIAM.
WOOD BALL
30(1¼)
6 (¼)
5 (¾)
19(13/16)
CUT-OUT SHAPE
6 (¼)
4 (⅛)
10 (⅜)
10 (⅜)

FINIAL
2 REQUIRED THUS

TUDOR DOLLS' HOUSE
SHEET 8

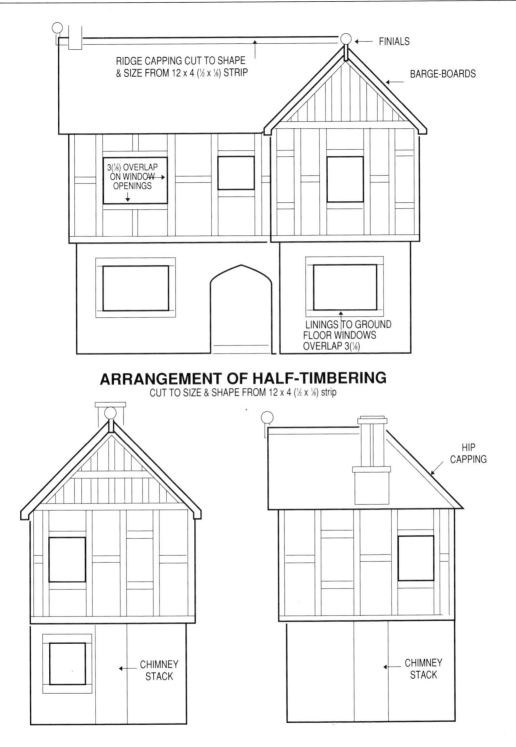

RIDGE CAPPING CUT TO SHAPE & SIZE FROM 12 x 4 (½ x ⅛) STRIP

FINIALS

BARGE-BOARDS

3(⅛) OVERLAP ON WINDOW OPENINGS

LININGS TO GROUND FLOOR WINDOWS OVERLAP 3(⅛)

ARRANGEMENT OF HALF-TIMBERING
CUT TO SIZE & SHAPE FROM 12 x 4 (½ x ⅛) strip

HIP CAPPING

CHIMNEY STACK

CHIMNEY STACK

TUDOR DOLLS' HOUSE

SHEET 9